Moral Practices

STUDIES IN ETHICS AND THE
PHILOSOPHY OF RELIGION

General Editor: D. Z. PHILLIPS

GOD AND THE SOUL
Peter Geach

MORALITY AND PURPOSE
J. L. Stocks

MORAL REASONING
R. W. Beardsmore

WITHOUT ANSWERS
Rush Rhees

THE FIVE WAYS
Anthony Kenny

MORAL PRACTICES
D. Z. Phillips/H. O. Mounce

GOD AND TIMELESSNESS
Nelson Pike

Moral Practices

by

D. Z. PHILLIPS *and* H. O. MOUNCE

SCHOCKEN BOOKS · NEW YORK

Published in U.S.A. in 1970
by Schocken Books Inc.
67 *Park Avenue, New York, N.Y.* 10016
© *D. Z. Phillips and H. O. Mounce* 1970
Library of Congress Catalog Card No. 78-100989

Printed in Great Britain

Contents

They said, 'You have a blue guitar,
You do not play things as they are.'

The man replied, 'Things as they are
Are changed upon the blue guitar.'

Wallace Stevens

Our clear and simple language-games
are not preparatory studies for a future
regularization of language—as it were
first approximations ignoring friction
and air-resistance. The language-
games are rather set up as *objects of
comparison* which are meant to throw
light on the facts of our language by
way not only of similarities, but also of
dissimilarities.

Wittgenstein

Preface

Readers may be interested in having an indication of the nature of the joint authorship of this essay. We have commented on and contributed to each other's work throughout, but sometimes special responsibility can be indicated.

The following sections have a single author: Sections 1, 2, and Appendix 1 (H.O.M.); Sections 3, 4, 9, and Appendices 2 and 3 (D.Z.P.).

Sections 5, 6 and 8 were written jointly. Section 7 can be divided as follows: the discussion of relativism and the comparison between Protagoras and Wittgenstein (H.O.M.); the rest of the Section (D.Z.P.).

We should like to make the following acknowledgements. Sections 3 and 4 consist in the main of the paper, 'Does It Pay To Be Good?' (D.Z.P.), first published in the *Proceedings of the Aristotelian Society*, Vol. LXV, 1964–5, and reprinted in *Ethics*, ed. by Judith Jarvis Thomson and Gerald Dworkin, 1968, and in *Sources in Contemporary Philosophy*, ed. by Frank Tillman, Harper and Row. We thank the Editor of the Aristotelian Society and Professor Tillman for permission to use the material here. Sections 5 and 6 consist in the main of the paper, 'On Morality's Having A Point' (D.Z.P. and H.O.M.), first published in *Philosophy*, October 1965. We thank the Editor for permission to use the material here. Appendix 2 is taken from two papers, 'Miss Anscombe's Grocer' and 'The Limitations of Miss Anscombe's Grocer', while Appendix

3 consists of the paper, 'The Possibilities of Moral Advice'. These papers appeared in *Analysis* in June 1968, January 1969 and December 1964, respectively. We are grateful to the Editor for permission to use the material here.

Finally, we wish to thank Mrs Janice Finch, Secretary to the Department of Philosophy at the University College of Swansea, for her readiness to type this essay, and for the care and industry with which she has done so.

D.Z.P. and H.O.M.

Swansea

Introduction

During the present century moral philosophers have been preoccupied with the relation between expressions of value and statements of fact. There can be little doubt that value judgements are related in some way to factual statements, since people often refer to facts in order to justify the value judgements they make. The question which has puzzled philosophers, however, is whether any value judgement can follow *logically* from the facts, can follow in such a way that someone who assents to the facts is bound in logic to assent also to the value judgement based upon them. This question is not an esoteric one in ethics. On the contrary, it can claim to be central, since answers given to it have determined views about the nature of moral judgements, what can be said about moral disagreement, and whether a man can be given any reasons why he should give attention to moral considerations at all.

At the moment, philosophical argument about the relation between facts and values seems to be dominated by two schools of thought. On the one hand, philosophers, such as R. M. Hare,[1] have argued that fact is logically distinct from value, that there is no logical inconsistency in denying a value judgement even though one has assented to the facts brought in support of it. On the other hand, in opposition to the view just stated, other philosophers, such as Philippa

[1] See R. M. Hare, *The Language of Morals*, O.U.P., 1952, and *Freedom and Reason*, O.U.P., 1963.

Foot,[1] have argued that certain facts entail the truth or falsity of moral beliefs, so that no moral agent who has assented to these facts can intelligibly deny the value judgements that follow from them. It has been suggested that the disagreement between these two schools of thought is not primarily a philosophical one. Indeed, doubt has been expressed as to whether there is any real disagreement involved at all. What is suggested is that both accounts of moral beliefs are right, since each account reflects the status of moral beliefs in different social backgrounds.[2] Since each account reflects different social conditions, any philosophical description of the relation between them as 'disagreement' is based on a misunderstanding. This essay does not share this view or follow its advice. The view involves a by-passing of the *philosophical* issues raised by the disagreements about the relation between fact and value. Far from thinking that philosophical discussion is redundant in this context, we feel that there is urgent need of it. This is because many philosophers are under the illusion of thinking that discussion in ethics must be conducted in terms of an either/or between the two views outlined. What we hope to show in this essay is that *neither* view concerning the relation of fact and value is satisfactory, and that progress in moral philosophy on this question, and the others we mentioned as being related to it, has as its precondition the recognition of this inadequacy.

[1] See Philippa Foot, 'When Is A Principle A Moral Principle?', *Aristotelian Society Proceedings*, Supp. Vol. XXVIII, 1954; 'Moral Beliefs', *Arist. Soc. Proc.*, 1958; 'Moral Arguments', *Mind*, 1958; 'Goodness and Choice', *Arist. Soc. Proc.*, Supp. Vol. XXXV, 1961.

See Alisdair MacIntyre, *A Short History of Ethics*, Routledge and Kegan Paul, 1967, p. 263 f.

1

Practice and Decision

We shall begin by considering the position of those who wish to distinguish sharply between fact and value. One difficulty confronting such a position is that for someone who holds a moral belief, certain facts seem already to possess moral import. For example, this seems to be true of the way in which we, within our society, use terms such as 'liar', 'murderer', 'generous', 'selfish'. To call a man a liar seems both to describe his character and to evaluate it; so that within our society these terms appear to be used in such a way that one cannot distinguish between their descriptive and evaluative function. To this a philosopher such as R. M. Hare might reply by saying that the impossibility referred to is psychological rather than logical. Although it is a fact that if one calls a man a liar within our society, one will be taken to disapprove of what he has done, it might be argued that one can nevertheless distinguish in logic between what he has done and the attitude expressed towards it; and one can imagine the former without the latter; one can imagine a description of lying that is purely factual.

To describe lying in factual terms, however, is more difficult than it might at first appear. One cannot, for example, simply describe lying as 'saying what is not the case', and if one adds 'with the intention to deceive', one has no longer confined oneself purely to factual terms, for 'deception' is as much a term carrying moral import as lying itself. Indeed, if one wants a purely factual term for lying it may be necess-

3

ary to invent one. Let us suppose that we have done so, that we possess the term 'Xing' which is a purely factual term for the act of lying. The possession of such a term should enable us, on Hare's account, to perceive the exact nature of value concepts, for what we are confronted by in a case of lying is an act that is properly described in purely factual terms. We are really confronted by the act of Xing, and the additional evaluative element that goes to make up our concept of lying is really projected on the act of Xing by us. It is therefore possible for a man not to apply this evaluative element if he should so decide. If, on the other hand, he should decide to apply it, then, according to Hare, he is bound as a matter of consistency to do so universally, to apply it to every case of Xing. He must adopt the *principle* that Xing is wrong, and he can allow exceptions to this principle only where he can offer a reason, in the form of a further principle, for doing so. On Hare's account, therefore, particular value judgements proceed from general principles that the individual has decided upon himself. One decides oneself that Xing is in general wrong, one adopts the general principle that one ought never to perform an act of Xing, and from this, by syllogistic reasoning, one can deduce the conclusion that a particular act, which falls under the principle, ought not to be performed.

Now it should be noticed that the premiss, Xing is wrong, in the above argument is a prescriptive judgement. Thus a prescriptive conclusion has been deduced from a prescriptive premiss, so that the appeal is from one prescriptive judgement to another. In opposition to this, we shall argue that a prescriptive judgement is justified *only by appealing to something that is not itself prescriptive*. To show the confusion involved in Hare's account we need to consider the nature of prescriptive judgements in greater detail.

It is important to distinguish between prescriptive judgements and mere commands. What distinguishes the one from the other is that a prescriptive judgement carries with it an appeal to authority, most commonly in the form of an established rule. Thus during a game of soccer one player might say to another, 'Stand back! You are off-side'. This utterance, though it takes the form of a command, is really to be distinguished from commands, for the utterance has the implication that the man to whom it is addressed already has a reason for carrying out what it says. The man who says 'Stand back! You are off-side', is not simply commanding the other to do what he wants him to do. He is as much pointing something out which, if the man himself had recognised it, would have led him to perform the prescribed action. We can see that this is so if we consider the statement, 'You are off-side'. Within association football there is a rule which says that a player will be called off-side and penalised if he receives the ball or is deemed to be interfering with play when there is no member of the opposing side between himself and the opposing goalkeeper. It is this rule that gives the order 'Stand back!' its prescriptive force and distinguishes it from a mere command. The order carries with it an appeal to a rule that the man in the off-side position recognises himself. What makes a judgement prescriptive is the appeal to a rule that is accepted or could be accepted by the man to whom the judgement is addressed. Without this rule, the judgement becomes a mere command, the mere attempt by one man to force another to do what he wants.

Having seen that a prescriptive judgement is related to a rule, we must now consider the precise nature of this relation. A prescriptive judgement can never *establish* a rule, but rather, a rule must already be accepted in order for a prescriptive judgement to be possible. Thus the statement of a rule is not itself prescriptive. If one says, 'Within association football there is a rule that no player, etc.' then one is not advocating anything, but simply stating what is the case within association football. Given that a person follows this rule, then on a particular occasion one can make a prescriptive judgement on the basis of it; one can tell a man that he ought to stand back if he does not wish to be off-side. It is to be noticed, however, that one is here advocating a particular act, where one can take for granted that

5

the man one is addressing is following a particular rule. One is *not* advocating obedience to the rule itself. Once again, it is only where one can *take for granted* that a man is following a rule that one can offer him a prescriptive judgement.

What we have said about the relation between a prescriptive judgement and a rule may be tested by means of an example. Let us suppose that a man A says to another B, 'You ought to wear a hat on Wednesdays'. When B asks why he should do so, A replies, 'Because it is the rule'. On B's asking to which rule A is referring, however, A simply replies, 'A rule I have decided on myself'. It is evident at once that A is simply misusing language in telling B that he *ought* to wear a hat on Wednesdays. Perhaps A has some obscure reason for wishing B to do what he says, but he should have expressed himself by saying, 'I *want* you to wear a hat on Wednesdays' or perhaps more strongly, 'Wear a hat on Wednesdays'. He is not entitled to express what he desires in the form of a prescriptive judgement except within the context of an accepted rule. A rule that a man has decided on himself is not such a rule at all.

It follows from the above account of prescriptive judgements that what Hare says is misguided, for, according to him, a particular prescriptive judgement can be justified by reference to a 'principle' that is itself a piece of advocacy, something one has decided on oneself. But, as we have seen, what distinguishes a prescriptive judgement from a mere command is that it can be justified by reference to something that does not itself need to be prescribed. For this reason, the account Hare gives is not really an account of prescriptive judgements at all. This conclusion is not evident immediately, because, as we shall try to show later, he places as the major premiss of his syllogisms statements resembling the things which really do serve to justify value judgements. If his view were correct, however, it would be possible to adopt any principle whatsoever as a major premiss, and derive genuine prescriptive judgements from it. Thus, one should be able to turn the utterance, 'You ought to wear a hat on Wednesdays' into a prescriptive judgement simply by deciding that all men ought to wear hats on Wednesdays. As we have seen, however, this is precisely what cannot be done. In order to make a prescriptive judgement, one must be able to appeal to something that does not itself need to be prescribed, and the principle that all men ought to wear hats on Wednesdays is not such a principle. But how do we know this? What right have we to rule this principle out in this context? In order to answer these questions we need to consider what within our society does serve to justify our particular value judgements.

It can be shown, we believe, that when we wish to justify our moral judgements or render them intelligible, we make use of such concepts as honesty, truthfulness, generosity, etc. These concepts have in consequence a special rôle in our society. It is extremely difficult to be clear about the character of this special rôle, however, because of the use philosophers sometimes make of such phrases as, 'Honesty is good', 'Lying is bad', 'Generosity is right', phrases that are rarely found in actual discourse. By their use of such phrases, philosophers give the impression that honesty, truthfulness and generosity are themselves the subjects of prescriptive judgements. They imply that in our society we need to arrive at a moral position in relation to these things. Now we can and do speak of adopting a moral position towards, say, capital punishment or pacifism, because these are both things about which people disagree, and we can imagine ourselves being asked to state our opinion about them, to say, for example, whether we consider capital punishment right or wrong. But it would be difficult to imagine ourselves being asked to give an opinion on truth telling or generosity. Someone confronted with a choice between telling the truth and helping a friend might ask whether or not a lie is justified *on this occasion*. Yet such a question could hardly arise were it not taken as a matter of course that a lie is normally to be condemned. It is therefore difficult to imagine the kind of situation in which a person would utter an expression like 'Truth telling is good'. It might be said

7

in the course of instructing a young child about how he should behave. But such an utterance could hardly raise an *issue*, for it would be difficult to know what someone who disagreed with it could mean.

Within our society, it is taken as a matter of course that a man should tell the truth rather than lie, respect life rather than kill, be generous rather than mean, and it is just because these things can be taken as a matter of course that it is possible for a man on a particular occasion to make a moral judgement or adopt a moral position. This is not to deny that particular decisions may influence a person's moral beliefs as much as any general moral beliefs he may hold. Nevertheless, unless some moral values were taken as a matter of course in a society, it is difficult to see how the occasion for particular decisions could arise. To say this is not to say that particular decisions must be viewed as the application of general rules. People do not normally assert that lying is bad; they assert that a particular act is bad because it involves lying. Here, however, it is apparent that lying is not itself the subject of a prescriptive judgement, for the reference to lying serves as a *justification*, and implies that to condemn an act as lying does not itself *need* to be justified. Thus it is just because in general we do *not* have to justify a condemnation of lying that we can on a particular occasion condemn a man for telling a lie.

When a philosopher uses a phrase like 'Lying is bad', however, he suggests that the above conclusion is not the case. He suggests that a moral position has been adopted towards lying, that we have decided, as it were, to come out against it. He speaks as if we have decided to come out against lying in a way comparable to that by which we might decide to come out against those who support capital punishment. If this were true, we could be then asked for the reasons which have led us to do so; we could be asked to justify our position. But a respect for truth is not the expression of a moral position. Rather, it is one of the things upon which we rely in supporting the moral positions we do adopt. We do not *decide* that lying is bad, because the alternative, that it is good, is not something we can bring before our minds. A phrase such as 'Lying is bad' must therefore be distinguished from a genuine expression of a moral position, for example, 'Capital punishment is wrong', where there is a real alternative which must be considered before our position can be properly expressed. The result of running the different cases together is to give the impression that there is nothing in morality to which we can appeal for justification, that everything is open to choice or decision. But this position is absurd, for choice is meaningless where there are no considerations upon which it can be based.

Someone may be puzzled by our contrast between phrases such as 'Lying is bad' and genuine moral positions. He may conclude that such phrases refer to something which is 'not genuine' or of little moral importance. Such a conclusion would, of course, be a bad confusion about what we are saying. What is being urged is that we should think of phrases such as 'Lying is bad' or 'Lying is wrong' not as expressions of a moral position, but as setting out one of the conditions under which a moral position can be expressed. They may be compared in this respect with a necessary proposition such as 'Red is a colour'. Someone who uttered this latter statement would not be making an assertion of fact, but stating a necessary truth which, if it conveyed information at all, could do so only about the meaning of the terms involved. Thus a person might say 'Red is a colour' in order to teach someone the meaning of the word 'colour'. We are suggesting that the phrase 'Lying is wrong' is also a necessary statement which, if it tells us anything at all, tells us about the meaning of 'morally wrong'. In saying that lying is wrong we are saying that what the term 'lying' describes is for us *necessarily* wrong. Lying is the kind of thing we apply the word 'wrong' to. This remark about the term 'wrong' is a *grammatical* remark, it marks out one of the limits of the term's use. Someone who did not apply the term in this way would have difficulty in understanding what we mean when we call something wrong.

9

If the above account of 'Lying is wrong' is accepted, it will enable us to explain why in our language there is no purely factual or descriptive term for lying. It is not that the term lying has no descriptive content, for clearly it has, but we only become aware of this descriptive content, we only learn to pick out acts of lying, in the course of learning the use of a term like wrong. From the outset, therefore, an act of lying has moral import for us. We do not first pick out an act of lying descriptively, and then place an evaluative element upon it by a separate act. Rather, from the beginning, we pick it out *as* something to be condemned. There is in this respect an analogy between the notion of a lie and the notion of off-side. It is from within the rules of football that a player first distinguishes an act as being off-side, and since these rules lay down that such an act is to be avoided, a player distinguishes an act of being off-side *as* something to be avoided from the outset. There is no gap between fact and value here, because what constitutes a fact—that a player is off-side—is distinguished from the beginning as having a value import. Similarly, since it is from within our use of a term such as wrong that we pick out acts of lying, an act of lying has a value significance for us from the beginning, and there can be no gap between determining that man has lied and concluding that he has done wrong. Part of the reason, at least, why we find it difficult to understand the transition from fact to value, is that we tacitly define a fact as something that does not possess moral import. Given this assumption, it follows by definition that from such facts we cannot infer any value conclusions. If it be remembered, however, that we understand something as a fact only in terms of the concepts we have learnt, and that these are sometimes value concepts, the transition from fact to value may no longer baffle us.

It is true, of course, that since the term 'lying' has a descriptive aspect, we can imagine it, as Hare suggests, as possessing this aspect alone. But Hare is wrong in supposing that whilst imagining the term 'lying' in a purely descriptive aspect, we can also come to a decision about whether lying is right or wrong. In order to ask whether something is right or wrong, we must abide by the rules governing the use of these terms. The application of the word 'wrong' to uses of lying is one of our criteria for the use of that term. When we consider lying in a purely descriptive aspect, then for the moment we step outside these criteria. Having done so, however, we can no longer ask whether a thing is right or wrong. We cannot seriously ask whether lying is wrong because in deciding whether an act is wrong we use lying as one of our criteria. One can convince oneself of this simply by trying to imagine the situation in which one would ask whether or not lying is right. One can imagine oneself asking whether a *particular* lie is justified, but if one asks whether lying in general is right, one finds oneself at a loss, not simply to answer the question, but to imagine the kind of consideration that would lead one to answer it. This is because one is no longer asking oneself a genuine question.

Perhaps this point can be made clearer by the following example. Let us consider a people who have the practice of promise keeping, and let us suppose that it is their sole moral practice. These people use the word 'ought' in what we should call a moral sense only in connection with the keeping of promises. Thus children are taught to do whatever they have undertaken to do, and sometimes to remind people who have not kept their word that they *ought* to do so. Their use of 'ought' is confined to this kind of circumstance. This practice of promise keeping is therefore comparable with our own, except that we are to imagine it as being self-contained, as being isolated from any other moral practice.

Now it is evident, we believe, that there can be no question of these people *deciding* that promises ought or ought not to be kept. Their moral judgements cannot be derived from a principle that they have arrived at by means of a decision. For by what procedure could they arrive at such a decision? It would have to consist in their asking themselves the question, 'Ought promises to be kept?' Yet within this society that question would be meaningless. These people are taught the use of 'ought' in its moral sense only with regard to keeping promises. The fact that a man has undertaken to do an action is their *criterion* for saying that the action ought to be done. To ask whether a man ought to keep his promises, that is, to ask whether a man ought to do what he has undertaken to do, is therefore, in this society, to involve oneself in a piece of nonsense, as if one were to ask, 'Ought one to do what one ought to do?' Of course, we can suppose these people to possess, as we do, a second sense of 'ought', of the kind that appears in the statement, 'You ought to keep your matches dry because it will pay you to do so'. On this conditional use of 'ought', it will be possible to ask whether promises ought to be kept, because it will then be equivalent to asking whether it *pays* one to keep them. This use of 'ought', however, is distinct from its moral use. We shall have occasion to stress this point later. We can continue to tell a person that he ought (in a moral sense) to perform a certain act even if it has been shown that it will *not* pay him to perform it. In terms of the moral use, therefore, it is evident that within this society it makes no sense even to ask, 'Ought promises to be kept?'

The above example enables us to conclude, we believe, that a moral judgement or decision is intelligible only where there are certain things that are not open to judgement or decision. What these certain things are which are not open to judgement or decision will depend on the moral practice of which one is a part. Thus, within the practice of promise keeping, one has a reason for saying that a man ought to perform an action if he has undertaken to do so; within that practice this is what constitutes a reason for such a judgement. But one has not decided oneself that this should count as a reason. What is to count as a reason or justification is determined by the practice of promise keeping to which one may belong, but which has not been brought into being by one's decision. It is only from within such a practice that one can speak at all of making a moral judgement or decision. This is why, from within the practice of promise keeping, one cannot ask whether a promise ought

12

to be kept. One would be asking whether that which justifies one's particular judgements is itself justified. And since one cannot even ask of a man who has promised to do something whether he ought to do it, it follows that for these people there can be no gap between fact and value. In our example, from *the fact* that a man has undertaken to do X, the judgement that he *ought* to do X will follow so inevitably that to question whether it follows will not even be intelligible.

2

Facts and Moral Conclusions

The position at which we have arrived by means of our criticism of Hare may be expressed in the following way. In order to make a moral judgement one must belong or be related to a moral practice within which, quite independently of any *decision* on the part of those who belong to that practice, certain facts entail that some things are right or wrong. For those who belong to a moral practice there must be certain occasions on which there is no gap between fact and value, on which such-and-such being right or wrong is entailed by such-and-such being the case. It is necessary, however, to distinguish between this position and one to which it bears an apparent resemblance, namely, the second school of thought outlined in the second paragraph of this essay.

Many philosophers, notably in this country Philippa Foot, who have maintained that a moral conclusion can be derived from a factual statement, have gone on to make far larger claims. They also want to maintain that a factual statement must entail the same conclusion for every moral agent, irrespective of the moral practices to which he belongs, and that moreover there is one set of facts from which any moral conclusion can be derived, so that any differences in moral judgements must be capable, ultimately, of being settled by reference to these facts. We cannot emphasise too strongly that these conclusions do *not* follow from the position for which we are arguing. We have argued that for everyone who is a moral agent certain facts will entail that some things are right or wrong, but from this it by no means follows that the same facts will entail that the same things are right or wrong for everyone who is a moral agent. To suppose that the one implied the other would be like supposing that because everyone has a mother, there is one mother whom everyone has. To maintain that within a moral practice certain facts will entail certain moral conclusions does not preclude the possibility of there being different moral practices within which the same facts entail different conclusions.[1]

The view that a given statement must entail the same conclusion for all moral agents is plausible only if we imagine a society that has a single moral practice or a set of moral practices that everyone shares. Thus, within our imaginary society, which has a single moral practice of promise keeping, any fact that has a moral significance for one moral agent, must have the same significance for another. This is because all moral agents within that society share in the same moral practice and must therefore share the same conception of what has moral significance. Let us, however, imagine a second society, B, comparable, let us suppose, with Sparta, in which private property has little significance, and in which a man is considered admirable if he succeeds in tricking another. The facts which have a moral significance for the members of the first society will clearly not have the same significance for the members of the second. Thus, for a member of society B, the fact that he has said he will repay money he has borrowed will be a fact without moral import. One can imagine his saying to a member of the first society, 'Granted that I have as a matter of fact said that I will repay the money, why is that a reason for supposing that I *ought* to repay it?' For such a person, who does not belong to the practice of promise keeping, saying that one will repay money has no relation to the judgement that one ought to repay it. It is perhaps of this

[1] For examples of this confusion in contemporary moral philosophy see Appendices 2 and 3.

kind of situation that Hare is thinking when he speaks of the gap between fact and value. He seems to us to be correct when he maintains that there is no means in logic by which the gap between fact and value can be bridged. For example, there is no argument or principle by which, in the case we referred to, a member of the first society can prove to a member of the second that he ought to repay the money. This follows from what has already been said about the practice of promise keeping. Within that practice what constitutes a proof that a man ought to repay money is just the fact that he has said he will do so. No other proof exists, nor, within that practice, is any other proof necessary. Should a man deny, however, that this does constitute a proof, which is precisely what a member of the second society does, then there is evidently nothing further that can be said to him. Hence there clearly is a sense in which, for a member of the second society, there exists a gap between his saying that he will repay the money and the judgement that the members of the first society would deduce from this. The view that a given fact must entail the same conclusion for all moral agents can be seen in consequence to be a mistaken one.

We want to emphasise no less, however, that the above conclusion does not imply that we have to fall back on the view put forward by Hare. On Hare's account, there is *never* a transition from fact to value except as a result of a decision. But this view is clearly mistaken. Although for a member of society B, the judgement that he ought to repay money does not follow from his having said that he will do so, it nevertheless does so follow *for the members of the first society*. It has not been shown that there is no transition from fact to value. What has been shown is that the transition which occurs within one moral practice need not do so within another. After all, this is no more than one would expect. Since the concept of a promise does not have the place within the second society that it has within the first, one would expect a member of the second society to consider it an arbitrary matter that the breaking of a promise is condemned. It will appear arbitrary to him because *his* moral judgements do not depend for their sense upon the use of this concept, but upon other apparently unrelated concepts. Thus, while he may understand what in a factual sense is involved in making a promise, the evaluative element in it will appear to him irrelevant, or, at best, a fact about the mental life, the attitudes, of those who employ the concept. In a comparable fashion, it will appear arbitrary to someone who is unacquainted with the rules of football that a player who is standing off-side should be told to stand back, and he may think it an odd fact about footballers that they do not happen to like a player's standing in this position. For this person, what has been said will appear to be connected only accidentally with what has occurred. On the other hand, someone who is acquainted with football knows that a player in an off-side position is told to stand back, not because people do not *happen* to like his standing in this position, but because it follows from the rules that he should not do so. *From within the rules of association football* the connection between a player standing in the position called off-side and his being told to stand back is not an accidental one; it will appear as such only to someone who does not know the rules of the game. Similarly, for a person who belongs to the practice of promise keeping, it will follow in certain circumstances that a man who has taken money ought to repay it. That it does not follow from another may simply indicate that in this person's life the moral practice of promise keeping has no part.

It is clear, then, that from within a moral practice certain moral judgements will follow from certain facts, and they will appear not to do so only to someone who does not share that practice. This conclusion follows from what was said in the first section of this essay. In order for a man to hold a moral position at all, there must be certain things it does not make sense for him to question. In our society, for example, it does not make sense to ask whether honesty is in general good, or murder bad, or generosity admirable. That this should be so is the condition for our making a moral judgement. If it did not follow as a matter of course that dishonesty was to be condemned, we should be unable to justify or render intelligible our condemnation of a dishonest action. For us, therefore, it must follow in normal circumstances that a man who has been dishonest has done something to be condemned. If someone could not see that it followed, this would be a sign that he did not share our moral practice. For this reason, the view of morality presented by Hare, in which a moral judgement can *never* follow from the facts, is like that of a man who has no moral practice of his own, and who can only look on at the moral practices of others. Only to such a person would the connection between a moral judgement and the facts always appear accidental. To such a person, moral judgements would be unintelligible.

In Sections 1 and 2 we have tried to show that two schools of thought which are prominent in contemporary moral philosophy are both mistaken. According to the first, moral judgements are connected only accidentally, by means of a personal decision, with what is the case. According to the second, there is one set of facts that will entail the correct moral conclusion to be adopted by a moral agent independently of the moral practices to which he belongs. We believe that the first position has been shown to be mistaken because there is a necessary relation for any moral agent between some sets of facts and certain things being right or wrong. We believe that the second position has been shown to be mistaken because the question of which set of facts is related to certain things being right or wrong will be settled for the agent by the moral practices to which he belongs.

3

Practice and Justification I

In the previous sections we have seen that in trying to understand how a transition from fact to value is possible in certain contexts, and in trying to understand also how, in certain other contexts, different moral conclusions can be drawn from the same set of facts, the notion of a moral practice played a central role. It was noted that particular judgements and conclusions arrived at within a moral practice, could only be justified or rendered intelligible if certain things are considered right or wrong without standing in need of further justification. It is these things which are our criteria for right and wrong in certain contexts, that go to make up our moral practices.

The above conclusions about moral practices are unacceptable to many contemporary moral philosophers. They agree with an assumption which they believe can be found in Plato's *Republic*, namely, that moralists are perpetrating a fraud in recommending justice as a virtue unless they can show the just man that justice constitutes a good for him. Their contention can be expressed not only with particular reference to justice, but more generally with reference to virtues as such. The view being advocated is that virtues can only be recommended if they constitute a good to the virtuous man. If virtues do not constitute such a good, they are frauds. It becomes essential, therefore, given this general assumption, to decide in general whether moral practices do constitute a good to the virtuous man; in other words, to decide whether it pays to be good.

It has been assumed that those who accept Thrasymachus's premiss—that injustice is more profitable than justice—and yet want to deny his conclusion—that a man who has the strength to get away with injustice has a reason to follow this as the best way of life—are in a dubious position. We shall argue that, on the contrary, it is the position just outlined which is dubious, one which, if adopted, reduces morality to prudence, and principle to policy.

According to the view of the justification of morality we have in mind, it is not denied that our reasons for acting in a certain way can be given in terms of moral considerations or moral principles, but the enquiry is pushed back a step further by asking why we have the moral rules we do. We have already noted in Section 1, however, how misleading it is to regard our moral practices as something we justify by appeal to wider considerations. Telling the truth rather than lying, respecting life rather than killing, being generous rather than mean, etc., are things which we take to be right as a matter of course. Some moral philosophers feel, however, that the pursuit of these practices needs to be justified by showing *why* we have these practices and *why* we pursue them. It is suggested sometimes that the moral practices we have can be justified because they lead to social cohesion, or because they satisfy the needs of society, or because they lead to the greatest happiness of the greatest number, and so on. What all these answers come to is that we observe the moral principles we have because it pays to do so. We believe these answers are radically mistaken, but it is not our intention to argue against them in this essay. Were we to do so, however, we should examine the relation of certain fundamental moral distinctions such as truth and falsity, justice and injustice, to the concept of community. We think it can be shown that we do not adhere to moral precepts in order that we might have a harmonious society, but that, on the contrary, the very notion of social existence has moral implications. The relation between moral rules and society is not a contingent one. P. H. Nowell-Smith[1] suggests that because these rules are so useful it has become difficult for us to imagine society without them. He says that robbers must have rules if robbery is to pay, whereas what ought to be said is that robbers must have rules if there is to be robbery. Our remarks here are sketchy and need working out, but apart from stating that the mistake of seeking a justification of moral practices as such in the ways suggested rests largely in a failure to take account of the moral implications in the very notion of society, we do not wish to pursue the point further. One reason for this is that we think it has been argued conclusively elsewhere,[2] and another is that we want to devote our attention to another kind of answer given to the question why we should pay any attention to moral considerations at all. The answer we have in mind attempts to reconcile a distinction between two senses of 'ought' which we think it essential to preserve: the sense of 'ought' in the statement, 'You ought to repay your debts' and the sense of 'ought' in the statement, 'You ought to keep your matches dry because it will pay you to do so'.[3] Recently, this answer has appeared in its most influential form in the writings of Philippa Foot,[4] and we intend discussing it in this and the following section in terms of her work.

Mrs Foot wants to find an answer to the question, 'Can we give anyone, strong or weak, a reason why he should be just?' Her answer to this question is that a man *needs* justice in his dealings with his fellow men whether he is strong or weak. Indeed, she thinks the need is so great that a man cannot get along without satisfying it. Judging from Mrs Foot's presentation of the matter, the question appears to be

---

[1] P. H. Nowell-Smith, *Ethics*, Penguin Books, 1954, pp. 226 f.

[2] See Peter Winch, 'Nature and Convention', *Arist. Soc. Proc.*, Vol. LX, 1959–60.

[3] Cf. Section 1, p. 12.

[4] See 'Moral Beliefs', *Arist. Soc. Proc.*, 1958.

straightforwardly empirical. We shall quote the relevant passage at length.

> Those who think that he can get on perfectly well without being just should be asked to say exactly how such a man is supposed to live. We know that he is to practise injustice whenever the unjust act would bring him advantage; but what is he to say? Does he admit that he does not recognise the rights of other people, or does he pretend? In the first case even those who combine with him will know that on a change of fortune, or a shift of affection, he may turn to plunder them, and he must be wary of their treachery as they are of his. Presumably the happy unjust man is supposed, as in Book II of the *Republic*, to be a very cunning liar and actor, combining complete injustice with the appearance of justice: he is prepared to treat others ruthlessly, but pretends that nothing is further from his mind. Philosophers often speak as if a man could thus hide himself even from those around him, but the supposition is doubtful, and in any case the price in vigilance would be colossal. If he lets even a few people see his true attitude he must guard himself against them; if he lets no one into the secret he must always be careful in case the least spontaneity betray him. Such facts are important because the need a man has for justice in dealings with other men depends on the fact that they are men and not inanimate objects or animals. If a man only needed other men as he needs household objects, and if men could be manipulated like household objects, or beaten into reliable submission like donkeys, the case would be different. As things are, the supposition that injustice is more profitable than justice is very dubious, although like cowardice and intemperance it might turn out incidentally to be profitable.[1]

In no way does Mrs Foot deny the logical possibility of the rogue she depicts succeeding and finding his villainy profitable. All she says is that things being as they are, it is as a matter of fact unlikely that justice pays. There is reason to doubt Mrs Foot's assessment of human conduct. Is it for nothing that people have wondered for so long why the wicked prosper? Her account is rendered plausible by the fact that she implies, though she says otherwise, that the happy unjust man will act unjustly whenever an opportun-

[1] See 'Moral Beliefs', *Arist. Soc. Proc.*, 1958, pp. 103–4.

ity arises. But why need we think that the unjust man always acts unjustly? He is more likely to conform to the practice of justice in most cases, and act unjustly only when it really pays to do so. Deceit depends to a large extent on a pre-established stock of goodwill. But there is little point in lingering over the factual question of whether a life of injustice is likely to profit a man. It is more important to note that despite the empirical character of Mrs Foot's argument, it has, underlying it, pre-suppositions concerning the nature of the importance we attach to moral actions.

In reply to the question why I should deal justly with my fellow men, Mrs Foot would reply, presumably, 'Because it is likely to pay or profit you to do so'. She is prepared to conceive of situations where things might be different; situations where human beings can be manipulated like inanimate objects or beaten into reliable submission like donkeys, but thinks that things are not like that. We should have thought that many a despotic sheikdom or the Nazi treatment of the Jews approximated to such a state of affairs. Mrs Foot takes no account of the fact that probabilities vary with the situation. In some cases, probability will be on the side of injustice proving profitable. For example, it is easy enough to imagine a ruler having such power over his subjects that any relaxing of his ruthless rule would lead to a loss of profit. It does not profit him to show a regard for the vast majority of his subjects. He simply keeps a strong, contented army. What is Mrs Foot to say about such a situation? If she wishes to be consistent she must say that since such a ruler is strong enough to get away with injustice, injustice and its profits are a sufficient reason for holding that the life the ruler leads is the best life he could lead. On the other hand, many people would want to say that the ruler was not living the best life he could lead, and that despite the fact that he found injustice profitable, he ought to deal justly with his subjects. One might put the matter provocatively by asking whether it profits a man to gain the whole world if he loses his own soul? Or, in case anyone should think that the previous question depends on one's holding religious beliefs, one could ask whether it profits a man to gain the whole world by committing despicable deeds? There seems to be a clash between two rival conceptions of what constitutes profit in a man's life. There is no dispute over the obvious profits which the ruler's injustice has brought him: wealth, gratification of his desires, ease, comfort, and so on. But a judgement is being passed on these profits which calls them unprofitable. This judgement is a moral judgement. Its possibility shows conclusively that the relevance of morality does not depend on whether it pays or not.

Mrs Foot has tried to find a non-moral justification for moral beliefs, and such an attempt always fails; it distorts the kind of importance which moral considerations have. It is due to her attempt to find a justification for adherence to justice in this way that Mrs Foot is led into such curious contradictions. She says: 'The reason why it seems to some people so impossibly difficult to show that justice is more profitable than injustice is that they consider in isolation particular just acts'.[1] Mrs Foot is not, as one might think at first reading the long passage we referred to, making the point that on the whole it is more profitable in each individual's life to act justly rather than unjustly. In order to appreciate her argument, one might imagine a scene often talked about from pulpits, namely, that of a man setting out on the journey of life. If he asks at the outset of the journey what he will need, what will benefit him on the journey, one answer is Justice. It is more likely that justice will benefit him on the journey than injustice. All will not run smoothly. Presumably, he must put up with an occasional unprofitable just act, since probability, where justice is concerned, is always on the side of profit. But this probability is not the probability of the course of any particular life, but the probability of the courses of people's lives in general. The individual who pursues justice may find that as a matter of fact justice has not paid in his life. Mrs Foot gives a striking example of this, namely, of a person being prepared

[1] ibid., p. 104.

to die rather than let an innocent man be convicted of a crime of which he is accused. She says of this person:

> For him it turns out that his justice brings disaster on him, and yet like anyone else he had good reason to be a just and not a unjust man,[1]

The good reason Mrs Foot refers to is the probabilities which faced such a man when he chose to practise justice. As it happens, his choice has led to disaster, but, as Mrs Foot says, 'like anyone else he had good reason to be a just and not an unjust man'. Notice the use of the past tense here—he had good reason—which again conjures up the picture of a man equipping himself with the essentials for the journey of life. But what of the man facing death because of his adherence to justice? Mrs Foot replies:

> He could not have it both ways and while possessing the virtue of justice hold himself ready to be unjust should any great advantage accrue.[2]

We are told 'that if a man is just it follows that he will be prepared, in the event of very evil circumstances, even to face death rather than to act unjustly'.[3] It seems to us, however, that on Mrs Foot's argument, such preparedness is unintelligible. A mysterious gap exists between one's initial choice of the way of justice, and one's acceptance of death as its result. If we ask, 'Why should we die?' and the answer given is, 'Because your practice of justice involved the risk of death', it can only be accepted on the assumption that our practice of virtue is carried on independently of the initial reason for its adoption, namely, the likelihood of profit. It is as if Mrs Foot were saying, 'Once you choose justice you must accept what justice brings'. If we ask why, the answer is simply, 'Because you are just'. The reason why we are just, namely, because we expect justice to pay, now seems to disappear in the background. The role of such a reason begins to appear more and more like murky

[1] ibid., p. 104.
[2] ibid.   [3] ibid.

3—MP * *

mythology: we are given a reason for accepting the consequences of just actions without reason. If, on the other hand, the likelihood of profit remains our reason for acting justly, we see no reason why, if there are people other than those whom Mrs Foot describes as 'too timid or too stupid to ask questions about the code of behaviour which they have been taught', there could not also be people who, at some time or other in their lives, question whether the initial justification for acting justly, namely, that it generally pays to do so, applies in their case. After all, the only relevance of the general survey of the results of virtue was to give the individual some idea of what was likely to be in store for him if he practised justice. But there may come a time when a man is better placed to assess whether justice pays in his own life than those who rely on general probabilities. Such a time is when a man faces death as the result of his policy to act justly. He no longer needs the general survey of probabilities. Death makes it always unprofitable to play the game which justice demands. Compared with all the profitable results which the pursuit of justice has led to in the past, death tips the balance. One cannot look to future events for redress, since death is not an event in the game, but the end of the game. Unless one is prepared to say that one must accept the path of justice even when one's reasons for choosing to walk it have now been proved to be false, one cannot give an intelligible account in terms of Mrs Foot's argument of why anyone should die for the sake of justice.

Mrs Foot assumes that if a man's just actions bring about his death, they have ended in disaster. She fails to see that for anyone concerned about justice, death for the sake of justice is not a disaster. The disaster for him would be to be found wanting in face of death, and to seek the path of injustice and compromise. Mrs Foot cannot give an account of anyone who sees death as a good; who dies for the sake of justice. She can only give an account of someone who dies as a result of justice, although, as we have tried to show, the justification for doing so is obscure. Death cannot appear in Mrs Foot's list of profits, since profit is always understood in terms of results in relation to the individual. Death cannot be profitable, since that in terms of which profitableness is to be assessed, namely, oneself, no longer exists. Mill, on the other hand, in his remarks on martyrdom, is able to show how one's own death can be regarded as a good, since for him, what makes it good is that it contributes to the greatest happiness of the greatest number. Mill says:

> The utilitarian morality does recognise in human beings the power of sacrificing their own greatest good for the good of others. It only refuses to admit that the sacrifice is itself a good. A sacrifice which does not increase, or tend to increase, the sum total of happiness, it considers as wasted.[1]

Whatever one thinks of Mill's answer, Mrs Foot, in terms of the views outlined, is precluded from making any use of it, since she says explicitly:

> Even if the general practice of justice could be brought under the motive of universal benevolence—the desire for the greatest happiness of the greatest number—many people certainly do not have any such desire. So that if justice is only to be recommended on these grounds a thousand tough characters will be able to say that they have been given no reason for practising justice, and many more would say the same if they were not too timid or too stupid to ask questions about the code of behaviour which they have been taught.[2]

In striking contrast to both Mill and Mrs Foot, Kierkegaard, in *Purity of Heart*, says of the death of Jesus:

> . . . nothing in the world has ever been so completely lost as was Christianity at the time that Christ was crucified . . . never in the world had anyone accomplished so little by the sacrifice of a consecrated life as did Jesus Christ . . . Was it not said by many intelligent men and women, 'The result shows that he has been hunting after phantasies; he should have married. In this way he would now have been a distinguished teacher in Israel'.

[1] *Utilitarianism*, ed. Mary Warnock, Fontana Series, 1962, p. 268.
[2] op. cit., p. 102.

And yet, eternally understood, the crucified one had in the same moment accomplished all! But the view of the moment and the view of eternity over the same matter have never stood in such atrocious opposition . . . Yet eternally understood, He had in the same moment accomplished all, and on that account said, with eternity's wisdom, 'It is finished'.[1]

Kierkegaard locates the value of the death of the martyr, not in the contribution which the death makes to something called the general happiness, nor in the fact that the martyr must put up with it as an unprofitable consequence of a policy which is on the whole profitable, but in the death itself. It is because the death of Jesus was what it was that Kierkegaard says that in dying Jesus had accomplished all. This brings us back again to the fundamental difference about the nature of profit in human action, about the sense in which it pays to be good.

It is tempting, but misleading, to think that the demands of decency can be shown to be worthwhile in the way in which an action might be shown to be prudential. What is misleading about it is brought out by Plato in the *Gorgias*. It is easy to think that Socrates is offering an external justification of moral practices. After all, he says explicitly that when actions are right they bring advantage, and when they are wrong, the reverse.[2]

This remark is easily misunderstood, however. This is illustrated by the ways in which Polus thinks Socrates's assertion can be falsified by what we have ventured to call the argument from witnesses or popular consent, and the argument from fear and intimidation.

First, let us consider the argument from witnesses or popular consent. By appealing to this argument Polus thinks that even a child can show Socrates to be mistaken. He appeals to recent history and cites examples of men who did evil things but who were happy nevertheless. Polus

[1] Søren Kierkegaard, *Purity of Heart*, trans. by Douglas Steere, Fontana Books, 1961, pp. 120–1.
[2] See Plato, *Gorgias*, trans. by W. Hamilton, The Penguin Classics, 1960, 470.

provides a list of crimes committed by Archelaus, a ruler of Macedonia, and comments on them ironically:

> So now, as the greatest criminal in the country, far from being the happiest Macedonian alive, he is the most miserable, and no doubt there are a number of Athenians, beginning with you, who would prefer to be any Macedonian, however obscure, rather than Archelaus.[1]

Polus is suggesting that only a fool would deny the obvious advantages which Archelaus enjoys, and that everyone in his heart of hearts would like those same advantages. He says to Socrates: '. . . in your heart you think as I do'.[2] But Socrates is quite unimpressed by this argument. He does not deny that as far as popular consent is concerned Polus will be able to provide an abundance of witnesses for his views: 'In the present case, for instance, practically the whole population of Athens, both native and alien, will agree with you that I am not speaking the truth, if you like to call them as witnesses.'[3]

But the truth in these matters is not arrived at by counting heads. Socrates is not seeking the kind of public acclaim for his views which Polus is emphasising. He wants rather to win Polus's assent through discussion.[4]

The second argument Polus uses is the argument from fear and intimidation. Socrates wants to say that a man is more miserable if his evil deeds go unpunished than if they are punished. Polus, on the other hand, wants to say that a man is more miserable if he is punished than if he escapes punishment. He thinks that Socrates's view is an extraordinary one and can be refuted easily.

> If a man is arrested for the crime of plotting a dictatorship and racked and castrated and blinded with hot irons, and finally, after suffering many other varieties of exquisite torture and seeing

[1] ibid., 471.

[2] ibid.   [3] ibid., 472.

[4] Socrates seems to have thought that if only the discussion is able enough and long enough he would get people to see the kind of demand moral considerations make on them. We shall have reason later to question this assumption and to examine its significance for ethics. See Section 6.

his wife and children suffer the same, is crucified or burnt at the stake, will he be happier than if he gets off, establishes himself as a dictator, and spends the rest of his life in power doing as he chooses, the object of envy and admiration to natives and foreigner alike? Is this what you maintain that it is impossible to prove untrue?[1]

Socrates replies, 'You're trying to frighten me with bogeys, my good Polus. You're no more proving me wrong than you were just now, when you appealed to witnesses'.[2] The fact that we would be afraid of suffering certain consequences of wrongdoing says nothing about what our moral attitude towards those consequences should be. The argument from fear and intimidation depends on the argument from popular consent. The horrors of punishment are paraded on the assumption that everyone would want to avoid such horrors, and therefore would want to avoid punishment.

Polus hopes to establish by means of his argument that advantage and disadvantage are contingently related to good and evil. If the good man's life is to his advantage, the connection between the goodness and the advantage is a contingent one. Socrates, on the other hand, seems to be arguing for some kind of necessary connection between goodness and advantage. It may seem that he is advancing the same thesis as we have found in Philippa Foot's writings. This, however, is to mistake the nature of Socrates's argument.

It might look at first as if Socrates and Polus were disagreeing over a straightforward matter of fact. Furthermore, it might seem that the point of view Socrates is advancing is a pretty impossible one. He wants to say that only the man who wills the good does what is to his advantage. It seems as if Polus can refute this easily simply by appealing to the facts. Indeed, it looks as if he has only to find one case of a wicked man flourishing to refute Socrates. But is this all the disagreement amounts to? If so, then we have to assume that Socrates is mistaken about facts which any Athenian

[1] ibid., 473. [2] ibid., 473.

could observe. But is Socrates denying any of the facts Polus mentions? He knows the history of Archelaus as well as Polus. In other words, the dispute between Polus and Socrates *is not a dispute about the facts*. It is as if Socrates said, 'Yes, Polus, I know all about the tyrant of Macedonia. I know all the facts about his crimes that you know, but I do not call that happiness'. The dispute between Socrates and Polus cannot be resolved by appealing to the facts. It is not like a dispute between two businessmen over whether a certain venture is profitable or not. There, although the businessmen disagree over the particular case, they are one in logic, that is, they share the same criteria of what constitutes profit. This is not true of Polus and Socrates. The reason why Polus thinks it so easy to refute Socrates is because he assumes that they share the same concept of happiness and advantage. But this is not the case. For Polus, worldly success and prudence determine what is to count as happiness and advantage. A man is happy in his eyes if he gets on in the world. When Socrates says that the right act is the advantageous act, he is insisting that you cannot understand what is to your advantage until you understand what rightness is. Similarly, when he says that the good man is the happy man he is saying that you do not understand what happiness is until you understand what goodness is. For Polus, what is good and right is determined by what popular consent decrees to be advantageous. For Socrates what is advantageous is determined by what is good and right. We see that Socrates's view is far removed from that of Philippa Foot. In her opinion, the facts must show that goodness is to a man's advantage. For Socrates, the facts are assessed in terms of the measure of goodness. Socrates is denying that one can give an account of morality in non-moral terms. He is the enemy of reductionism in ethics. In the *Gorgias* he is concerned to distinguish between the kind of role played by moral considerations in action and the kind of role played by prudential considerations. This distinction is extremely important. We shall try to develop it further in the following section of the essay.

4

Practice and Justification II

In considering what might be meant by saying that it pays to be good, the differences between Mill and Mrs Foot are relatively unimportant, for each locates the value of just action in considerations which refer beyond the action itself to its results. Kierkegaard condemns this attempt at justifying morality in non-moral terms, and it matters little whether the justification concerned refers to the benefits of one or to the benefits of all, since what is being criticised is the view of moral action which these positions imply. We want to consider the force of Kierkegaard's criticisms.

Kierkegaard believes that something can be said in general about all actions performed because of our moral beliefs. He says that such actions must be performed from a love of the good. He contends that to will the good is to will one thing. Before considering the relation of his position to Mrs Foot's argument in greater detail, it is advisable to show that Kierkegaard's position is a philosophical one. This is partly because the talk about 'willing one thing' might tempt one to think that Kierkegaard's answer is an empirical one. When we are told that to will the good is to will one thing, we might ask what the one thing is: is it this, that, or the other thing? Kierkegaard describes the task awaiting anyone who interprets his answer in this way:

> If one considers this matter properly must he not first consider,
> one by one, each goal in life that a man could conceivably set up
> for himself, mentioning separately all of the many things that a

man might will? And not only this; since each of these considerations readily becomes too abstract in character, is he not obliged as
the next step to attempt to will, one after the other, each of these
goals in order to find out which is the single thing he is to will,
if it is a matter of willing only one thing?[1]

Philosophically, such enumeration will never bring one
to see the importance of moral action, not because the task
is endless, but because the enquirer 'at the outset . . . took
the wrong way and then continued to go further and further along this false way'.[2]

Kierkegaard is not interested in the specific objects of
people's wills, but with what it means to will the good. His
'one thing' is not some thing or other. Furthermore, if we
separate the moral objects of people's wills from the multi-
tude of things which people will, it cannot be said that
Kierkegaard is interested in any of these in particular
either; that is, he is not concerned with this or that moral
principle or belief. When he says that to will the good is to
will one thing, he is concerned with the form of morality
and not with its content. He is well aware of the distinction
between what things are good and the concept of moral
goodness. Kierkegaard recognises that moral philosophy is
concerned solely with the latter; that it is not the business
of philosophy to advocate moral beliefs, but to ask what it
means to have moral beliefs. Hence the point of his remark
that his 'talk is not inquisitive'.[3]

Kierkegaard's point, then, that to will the good is to will
one thing, is a philosophical and not an empirical observation. Yet, why does Kierkegaard choose to express it in this
way, by saying that to will the good is to will *one* thing?
Why not two things, three things, or many things? He does
so in order to stress that a moral action has a certain unity,
that its importance is internally related to the action itself.
In so far as the importance of the action is externally related to
the action, Kierkegaard says it is an instance of what he calls
'double-mindedness'. It is at this point that Kierkegaard's

[1] op. cit., pp. 47–8.
[2] ibid., p. 48.   [3] ibid., p. 161.

argument becomes relevant as a criticism of Mrs Foot's position, since she says that the reason we commend justice as a virtue is because on the whole it pays one to pursue it. Kierkegaard shows that if the reason for moral actions is said to be beyond the actions themselves, it follows that actions are morally indifferent for anyone who acts according to this rule. We want to elaborate on Kierkegaard's arguments.

Actions are morally indifferent for a person when it no longer matters to him whether he does one thing rather than another. If one claims to have moral beliefs or to act according to moral principles, it does make a difference to one whether one does one thing rather than another. We shall try to show how, if one thinks that non-moral reasons can be given for moral actions, the attempt at so explaining moral beliefs leads one to deny them.

Let us assume that the point of virtue is its profitableness. We wish to say that if one gives alms to a beggar in order to impress one's employer and obtain an increase in salary, it does not make a difference to one whether one does one thing rather than another. At first this seems absurd. Of course one's actions made a difference to one: they made a difference to one's employer's opinion of one, and they made a difference to one's salary. One's action was a purposive action; it functioned as means to one's end. The end is all important, the means relatively unimportant. *As it happened*, the means turned out to be giving alms to a beggar, but helping a blind man across the street, breaking up an uneven dogfight, flattery, or a thousand other things, might have done just as well in securing the desired end. Whether one does this or that is contingently related to the end one is aiming at.[1] The same conclusions follow if one considers the person who performs 'just' actions, not for the sake of profit, but to avoid punishment for failing to do so.

[1] Mrs Foot herself has argued that what is to count as a moral principle cannot be a contingent matter. See 'When Is A Principle A Moral Principle?', *Arist. Soc. Proc.*, Suppl. Vol. XXVIII, 1954. Our objections are to the way she has tried to develop her arguments there in later papers.

As Kierkegaard says of him, *'He does continually what he would rather not do'.*[1]

To hold a moral principle, it is essential that the principle be distinguishable from what a man wants. Mrs Foot, on the other hand, thinks that 'the nature of justice can be shown to be such that it is necessarily connected with what a man wants'.[2] We are not denying the possibility of the convergence of duty and desire in given instances, but it must always be possible to specify what would constitute a clash between one's moral beliefs and one's desires. If one provides a non-moral reason for moral action, whether it be pleasure, happiness, or profit, as long as the pleasure, happiness or profit envisaged is one's own, such a clash is inconceivable. This is true of any attempt to explain moral conduct as means to some personal end. One must distinguish between moral beliefs and the expedient use of moral beliefs. Kierkegaard speaks of the man for whom expediency and profit are the rule in *Either/Or*. He is called, 'the lover of the momentary', 'the man whose interest is in the particular', 'the sensualist', and so on. The portrait is a deliberate caricature, but is meant to illustrate the lack of consistency involved in a life of expediency.

> One is struck by seeing a clown whose joints are so limber that all necessity for maintaining the human gait and posture is done away. Such are you in an intellectual sense, you can just as well stand on your head as on your feet, everything is possible for you . . . . A man who has a conviction cannot at his pleasure turn topsy-turvy upon himself and all things.[3]

There is a deceptive consistency about Mrs Foot's picture of the just man. She is able to say that, 'The man who has the virtue of justice is not ready to do certain things'.[4] Yet, we must remember her fundamental reason for thinking this so, namely, that it is unlikely to pay a man to do

[1] ibid., p. 76.
[2] op. cit., p. 101.
[3] Søren Kierkegaard, *Either/Or*, trans. by Walter Lowrie, O.U.P., Vol. II, p. 14.
[4] op. cit., p. 104.

these things. We do not see how Mrs Foot can distinguish between the man who loves justice, and the man who performs 'just' actions because it pays to do so. Even if we accept the argument that in fact justice pays, we can imagine people performing just actions for other reasons, namely, for the sake of the actions themselves. Would Mrs Foot find such conduct morally praiseworthy? If so, what would be her reasons for calling such conduct moral?

Kierkegaard wants to say that all things are not possible for a man who has moral beliefs. Mrs Foot would like to say the same, but she employs a concept of possibility which does not allow her to say so. True, if we are performing an action because it brings us profit, it is not open to us to do anything which will lose us that profit. So far this is simply the model of all purposive action: if you want *A*, you must do *B*, *C* and *D*. But this has nothing to do with morality. It may be that in order to profit in life we have to keep our promises, tell the truth, act justly, show kindness, and so on. But it may be the case that what profits us is breaking our promises, lying, injustice, and callousness. If all we are concerned about is what profits us, we shall choose the course which is most likely to bring us these profits. Mrs Foot says that justice is profitable, but that has nothing to do with morality. If injustice were profitable, she would have to advocate pursuing it.

Let us consider a concrete example. A person's father has committed murder, he knows that he has, and the police have come for him. He refuses to hand over his father to them. Someone asks him why he refuses to do so, to which he replies, 'I can't.' What kind of impossibility is involved in the answer? According to Mrs Foot, the fundamental reason for his action, assuming we think it moral, is the place which this action has in the general profitableness of moral actions. So he does not hand over his father to the police because, generally speaking, this kind of action pays. The impossibility of his action is a contingent matter. There is nothing in the action itself which makes it impossible for him to do it, since if it did not pay not to do it, he would do it. This is a travesty of the reasons he would give for not handing his father over to the police. What he would say, in fact, would be, 'Because he is my father'. Mrs Foot would not be content with this answer. She says that 'the affection which mothers feel for children, and lovers for each other, and friends for friends, will not take us far when we are asked for reasons why a man should be just'.[1] Mrs Foot's answer, namely, profit, takes us away from moral considerations altogether. The impossibility of the person's being able to give up his father to the police does not depend on profitableness or unprofitableness, but on what it means to give up one's father to the police. It is *that* that he could never do, whereas the man who does not do it because of profit *could* do it; it is simply a contingent matter that he does not. Furthermore, if we try to show one of Mrs Foot's thousand tough characters why he should not leave his father destitute in his old age, we shall never do so by convincing him that it will profit him to do so, or that such actions generally profit people. Perhaps, as a result of the latter arguments, he decides to look after his father. No matter, for what we have taught him to have is a regard for profit, not a regard for his father. If Mrs Foot said that this is but another instance of concentrating on particular just acts, we should reply by saying that it is only by taking account of actual situations in which men make stands for their moral beliefs that the nature and importance of such beliefs come to be appreciated.

A word about remorse, a neglected concept in contemporary moral philosophy, is relevant in this context. No analysis of moral action in terms of the means-ends distinction can account for remorse, unless one believes with Nowell-Smith that it does not differ importantly from embarrassment.[2] On Mrs Foot's account, we should not leave our fathers destitute in their old age because it is highly probable that it will not pay us to do so. Suppose that we go on regardless, and then find out that she is right. We may feel frustrated because we have not achieved the

[1] ibid., p. 102. [2] op. cit., p. 26.

profit we had hoped to gain, in much the same way as we might feel frustrated at not getting a job. But this is far from remorse. One cannot explain remorse unless one realizes that the just man cares about just actions. Mrs Foot's picture of the man who possesses the virtue of justice is a caricature: it is a picture of a person who performs actions which are just in their externalities. A man can perform 'just' actions without being just. If one thinks of moral goodness as a function of man in much the same way as cutting well is the function of a knife, one cannot account for praise and blame in moral discourse.[1] We do not blame the knife for being a bad knife, but we do blame a person for a bad action, unless his reasons for the action show that our assessment of what the action amounted to was mistaken. The reasons we have for acting place our actions in intelligible contexts where they can be judged by other people. If our actions were mere means to our ends, it would be impossible to feel remorse because of them, but since they are important in themselves as far as morality is concerned, what we do and why we do it can occasion remorse; remorse because we have committed such despicable deeds. Actions are ruled out for the just man, not because they would not profit him, but because they are what they are. If unjust actions are performed by the just man he feels remorse because he discovers that he is the kind of man for whom such actions were not ruled out after all. The means-ends distinction, then, which plays such an important part in Mrs Foot's argument, is foreign to morality. Kierkegaard asks the man striving to be decent:

> What means do you use in order to carry out your occupation? Are the means as important to you as the end, wholly as important? Otherwise it is impossible for you to will only one thing, for in that case the irresponsible, the frivolous, the self-seeking, and the heterogeneous means would flow in between in confusing and corrupting fashion. Eternally speaking, there is only one means and

[1] See J. L. Evans, 'Grade Not', *Philosophy*, January 1962. We shall discuss the attempt to compare moral goodness with the goodness of a knife in greater detail in Section 5.

there is only one end: the means and the end are one and the same thing. There is only one end: the genuine Good; and only one means: this, to be willing only to use those means which genuinely are good—but the genuine Good is precisely the end.[1]

Kierkegaard's point is substantially the same as Kant's remarks on the heteronomy of the will. But one does not have to go outside the present century to find a powerful attack on the alleged importance of the means-ends distinction for morality. We have in mind the neglected, but important, writings of J. L. Stocks. Stocks questions, quite rightly, the adequacy of the Aristotelian notion of rational action as an account of morality. But he does not suggest that the distinctive contribution of morality to action consists in adding a further purpose to the action, or in superseding purposes already given. Morality operates as 'an additional principle of discrimination . . . by setting a differential value on features which to purpose were indifferent or equal in value'.[2] Once this is recognised, the inadequacies of the means-ends distinction are soon apparent.

The moral attitude is essentially a concern for the rightness of action . . . morality requires that all means shall be justified in some other way and by some other standard than their value for this or any end: that however magnificent is the prospect opened out by the proposed course of action, and however incontestable the power of the means chosen to bring this prospect nearer, there is still always another question to be asked: not a question whether in achieving this you will not perhaps diminish your chances of achieving something still more important; but a question of another kind. 'There is a decency required,' as Browning said, and this demand of decency is prepared to sacrifice, in the given case, any purpose whatever.[3]

Stocks illustrates his point with the simple example of someone who discovers a quick and legally admissible way of making money. The means are in his power, and the end

[1] *Purity of Heart*, p. 177.
[2] J. L. Stocks, *Morality and Purpose*, ed. with an Introduction by D. Z. Phillips, Routledge and Kegan Paul, 1969, p. 27.
[3] ibid., p. 77.

in view is undeniably profitable. But morality says, 'Not that way'. Nothing is denied that the purposive outlook asserts: the relative lack of effort needed, the rich recompense expected, the calculation involved. But given the proposed action, morality sees in it a barrier which cannot be passed. To the observer who has eyes only for the end and the easiest methods of attaining it, the moral judgement will seem arbitrary, and close to madness. The judgement can only be understood by those who have a regard for decency, or, as Kierkegaard would have said, 'a love of the good'.

But what of those who wish to reconcile the purposive outlook with morality? Could they not say that the non-moral end of the above example is subordinated to a higher *moral* end? To this suggestion, Stocks has the final answer:

> I know that there are many who will tell me that my difficulty is imaginary; that there is a moral aim and purpose, which is the ultimate overriding purpose of life; that this man, who rejects a safe and legally admissible means of enriching himself, rejects it because he is after something more important than that, with which in the given circumstances that conflicts. He is seeking, they will perhaps say, his own spiritual development and perfection, to which I might reply that the act must first be shown to be right now before it can be relied upon to build up righteousness in the future; and—more relevantly to our present enquiry—that there may well be such an aim, and it may well be considered more important than riches, but that it is after all only an end, like any other, a possible result of action, and that it falls, with all other ends, under the inflexible moral rule that it may not be pursued by any and every means. Morality may call on a man at any moment to surrender the most promising avenue to his own moral perfection.[1]

It is to Mrs Foot's credit that there is little talk of the goal of moral perfection as the point of moral conduct in her writings. On the other hand, it is not at all clear to us that the profit she envisages as the result of just conduct is moral profit at all. Judging from the long passage from her paper which we have made the basis of our objections, the opposite seems to be the case. That being so, let us imagine

[1] ibid., pp. 28-9.

a person who refused to take Mrs Foot's advice at the outset of life about the probability of profit being on the side of justice. Certainly, at that early time, he had good reason to choose justice rather than injustice, but, being a gambler by nature, he chose injustice. As it happened, things went well for him. He profited in every way he wished to profit. Now, on his death-bed, he looks back over his life with relish: 'It was certainly a lucky day for me when I gambled against the odds on lying, cheating, swindling, and betraying, paying off'. Many would want to say that what this man did was wrong. For them the fact that in facing death he shows no remorse is but an additional mark against him. But Mrs Foot can give no account of this judgement. She must admit that he has in fact lived the best life he could have. Her only consolation is that such a man, like everyone else, had good reason to choose justice rather than injustice. But he chose injustice!

The man who chooses justice may not profit as our rogue has done. None of the things that Mrs Foot envisages as probably coming his way may prove to be his lot. Nevertheless, since his regard for decency does not depend on such probabilities being realised, in the only sense relevant to morality, he has accomplished all.

Socrates reaches similar conclusions in the *Gorgias*. He says there that the good man cannot be harmed.[1] If one takes this to be a straightforward factual claim it is false. We know of scoundrels who flourish, and of good men who are plunged into distress. Socrates is not denying these facts. He is arguing that the good man is never justified in saying that his lot is harmful, in the sense that what has occurred has rendered doing good pointless. Socrates says that if a man does good he can expect to have good done in return to him. At first, this looks like a policy of prudence: I'll do good to you if you do me some good in return. But we have already seen that actions performed under such conditions cannot be said to be morally praiseworthy in the first

[1] For a stimulating discussion of this question see Peter Winch, 'Can A Good Man Be Harmed?', *Arist. Soc. Proc.*, Vol. LXVI, 1965–6.

41

place. But this interpretation cannot be given to Socrates's remarks. We know this because Socrates says that a good man has no right to be dissatisfied with his lot, *no matter what his lot is*. This distinguishes his case from that of the prudential man. The latter's conduct is determined by the expectation of a certain kind of repayment. If this repayment is not forthcoming, the necessary and sufficient conditions for performing the action are removed. The disagreement between Socrates and Callicles is not a disagreement over the probable consequences of pursuing the good. He says to Callicles, 'Don't tell me once more that my life will be at the mercy of anyone who pleases, or I shall repeat that in that case I shall be the innocent victim of a villain; nor yet that I shall be stripped of my possessions, or I shall tell you again that the man who strips me will gain nothing from his spoil.'[1] Socrates is not denying that he might be persecuted. On the contrary, he believes he will be. Callicles does not understand this and confuses Socrates's confidence with complacency. He says, 'You seem to me, Socrates, as confident that none of these things will happen to you as if you were living in another world and were not liable to be dragged into court, possibly by some scoundrel of the vilest character'.[2] That this is a misunderstanding is shown by Socrates's explicit remark, 'I should be a fool, Callicles, if I didn't recognise that in this state anything may happen to anybody'.[3] Yet, having said this, Socrates is able to go on to say without contradiction that all will be well. He would be ashamed only if his death was the result of forsaking the good. But if he dies for the sake of the good and because he refuses to play the game for which sophistry equips one, he will feel no shame.

We can now see why Socrates says that the good man cannot be harmed. He refuses to call anything which results from a pursuit of the good harmful. It is not the world which is to determine what is harmful. On the contrary, harm, for Socrates, is to be measured by the extent of a man's deviation from the good.

[1] op. cit., 521.   [2] ibid., 521.   [3] ibid., 521.

We can also see something now of what Socrates meant by saying that the good man has good done to him. He is not suggesting that the pursuit of goodness is a conditional policy. Neither is he saying that one's own moral development is the aim of one's actions. Rather, he is saying that goodness is its own reward. Socrates says that the man who trains someone in a skill may or may not be paid. The training and the payment are externally related to each other; they can be understood independently of each other. A trainer may teach a man to run so quickly that he runs away with the fee. But there is no fear of the good man going unpaid, since the payment is internally related to the exercise of goodness. He cannot be at a loss if the regard for goodness remains with him. He does not feature prominently, if at all, in this regard. It is a regard for goodness not for himself. If one wishes to speak of payment or reward at all in this context, one must remember that their meaning is inseparably bound up with the individual's regard for the good and his desire to be a worthy vehicle of it.

5

The Revival of Ethical Naturalism

Let us recall again the conclusions we reached in Sections 1 and 2. There we saw that it is wrong to assume that evaluative conclusions cannot be drawn from any set of facts, since given certain moral practices, certain facts do have moral import. We also saw, however, that it is wrong to assume that the same moral conclusions will always follow from a given set of facts, since given different moral practices, the same facts will have different moral import. In Sections 3 and 4 we have been considering one reaction to these conclusions. The reaction in question rests on a desire to give some justification of moral practices as such. We saw how this can take the form of an attempt to show that it pays to be good. A reason is thus given to us which is supposed to tell us why we should adhere to moral practices. Far from doing this, however, we saw how the attempt to justify or advocate moral action in non-moral terms distorted the kind of importance moral considerations often have, and blurred the distinction between morality and prudence. In the present section and the one which follows it, we want to consider another, but closely related, reaction to the above mentioned conclusions. It is a reaction in particular to the second conclusion we reached, namely, that where moral practices differ, facts will have different moral import. Some philosophers seem unsatisfied with this philosophical readiness to recognise that there are a multiplicity of different moral practices, some of them opposed to each other. For reasons we shall try to make clear, they want to reduce what we regard as an irreducible variety in moral practices to some kind of unity. We turn now to an examination of their attempts to do so.

In an article published in 1958, Miss Anscombe argued that moral philosophy must await the development of an adequate philosophy of psychology.[1] What is needed, she argued, is an enquiry into what type of characteristic a virtue is, and, furthermore, it was suggested that this question could be resolved in part by exploring the connection between what a man ought to do and what he *needs:* perhaps man needs certain things in order to flourish, just as a plant needs water; and perhaps what men need are the virtues courage, honesty, loyalty, etc. Thus, in telling a man that he ought to be honest, we should not be using any special (moral) sense of ought: a man ought to be honest just as a plant ought to be watered. The 'ought' is the same: it tells us what a man needs.

The implications of the above arguments have been worked out in some detail by Philippa Foot in the papers we have had occasion to mention already.[2] The attack on the naturalistic fallacy which they involve has been welcomed by a contemporary defender of Utilitarianism.[3] Strong support for a deductive argument from facts to values has come from Max Black,[4] while agreement with this general approach in ethics can be found in the work of von Wright who, in discussing the varieties of goodness, denies that there is a peculiar *moral* sense of 'good'.[5] Also,

---

[1] G. E. M. Anscombe, 'Modern Moral Philosophy', *Philosophy*, Jan. 1958.

[2] See 'Moral Beliefs', 'Moral Arguments', and 'Goodness and Choice'. For references see p. 2 n. 1.

[3] See Mary Warnock's Introduction to *Utilitarianism*, Fontana Books, 1962, p. 31.

[4] Max Black: 'The Gap Between "Is" and "Should"', *Philosophical Review*, April 1964. A criticism of this paper can be found in Appendix 3 of this book.

[5] G. H. von Wright, *The Varieties of Goodness*, Routledge and Kegan Paul, 1963.

contemporary philosophers have been prompted to explore the connections between morality and prudence,[1] and even to express the hope that past masters will have a salutary influence on the future relationship between philosophy and psychology.[2] It seems fair to say that Miss Anscombe's contentions have helped to produce a climate of opinion, a way of doing moral philosophy. For this reason, it is all the more important to expose the radical understanding involved in them.

One important thread running through the developments we have indicated is that it has come to be thought important once again in ethics to ask for the point of morality. Why does it matter whether one does one thing rather than another? Surely, it is argued, if one wants to show someone why it is his duty to do something, one must be prepared to point out the importance of the proposed action, the harm involved in failing to do it, and the advantage involved in performing it. Such considerations simply cannot be put aside. On the contrary, the point of moral conduct must be elucidated in terms of the reasons for performing it. Such reasons separate moral arguments from persuasion and coercion, and moral judgements from likes and dislikes; they indicate what constitutes human good and harm.

If we take note of the role of reasons in morality, we shall see that not anything can count as a moral belief. After all, why does one regard some rules as moral principles, and yet never regard others as such? Certainly, we *can* see the point of some rules as moral principles, but in the case of other rules we cannot. How is the point seen? There is much in the suggestion, as we have seen, that it is to be appreciated in terms of the background which attends moral beliefs and principles.[3] When rules which claim to be moral rules are

[1] See R. S. Peters and A. S. Phillips Griffiths, 'The Autonomy of Prudence', *Mind* 1962.

[2] See Richard Wollheim's Introduction to Bradley's *Ethical Studies* O.U.P. Paperback Edn. 1962, p. xvi.

[3] See Mrs Foot's paper, 'When Is A Principle A Moral Principle?' *Arist. Soc. Proc.* Supp. Vol. XXVIII, 1954.

devoid of this background we are puzzled. We do not know what is being said when someone claims that the given rule is a moral rule.

Normally, we do not speak of these backgrounds when we express and discuss moral opinions. It is only when we are asked to imagine their absence that we see how central they must be in any account we try to give of morality. Consider the rules, 'Never walk on the lines of a pavement', and 'Clap your hands every two hours'. If we saw people letting such rules govern their lives in certain ways, taking great care to observe them, feeling upset whenever they or other people infringed the rules, and so on, we should be hard put to understand what they were doing. We fail to see any point in it. On the other hand, if backgrounds are supplied for such rules, if further descriptions of the context in which they operate are given, sometimes, they can begin to look like moral principles. Given the background of a religious community, one can begin to see how the rule, 'Never walk on the lines of a pavement', could have moral significance. Think of, 'Take off thy shoes for thou art on holy ground', and its connections with the notions of reverence and disrespect. It is more difficult, though we do not say it is impossible, to think of a context in which the rule, 'Clap your hands every two hours', could have moral significance. Our first example shows how we can be brought to some understanding of a moral view when it is brought under a concept with which we are familiar. By linking disapproval of walking on the lines of a pavement with lack of reverence and disrespect, even those not familiar with the religious tradition in question may see that a *moral* view is being expressed. Such concepts as sincerity, honesty, courage, loyalty, respect, and, of course, a host of others, provide the kind of background necessary in order to make sense of rules as moral principles. It does not follow that all the possible features of such a background need be present in every case. The important point to stress is that unless the given rule has *some* relation to such a background, we would not know what is meant by calling it a moral principle.

47

The above conclusion follows from a more extensive one, namely, that commendation is internally related to its object. Mrs Foot, for example, suggests that there is an analogy between commendation on the one hand, and mental attitudes such as pride and beliefs such as 'This is dangerous' on the other. One cannot feel proud of *anything* any more than one can say that *anything* is dangerous. Similarly in the case of commendation: how can one say that clapping one's hands every two hours is a good action? The answer is that one cannot, unless the context in which the action is performed, for example, recovery from paralysis, makes its point apparent.

Certainly, those who have insisted on the necessity of a certain conceptual background in order to make sense of moral beliefs and moral judgements have done philosophy a service. They have revealed the artificiality of locating what is characteristically moral in a mental attitude such as a pro-attitude, or in a mental activity such as commending. They have shown the impossibility of making sense of something called 'evaluative meaning' which is thought of as being externally or contingently related to its objects. One could have a pro-attitude towards clapping one's hands every two hours, and one could commend one's never walking on the lines of a pavement, but neither pro-attitude nor commendation would, in themselves, give a point to such activities. We reached similar conclusions in Section i of this essay.

If the point of virtues is not to be expressed in terms of pro-attitudes or commendations, how is it to be brought out? It has been suggested that this could be done by showing the connection between virtues and human good and harm. But if we are not careful, we may, in our eagerness to exorcise the spirit of evaluative meaning, fall under the spell of the concept of human good and harm, which is an equally dangerous idea. Unfortunately, this has already happened, and much of the current talk about human good and harm is as artificial as the talk about 'attitudes' in moral philosophy which it set out to criticise.

The point of calling an action (morally) good, it is suggested, is that it leads to human good and avoids harm.
Further, what is to count as human good and harm is said
to be a *factual* matter. Thus, one must try to show that there
is a logical connection between statements of fact and statements of value, and that the logical gap supposed to exist
between them can be closed. Men cannot pick and choose
which facts are relevant to a moral conclusion, any more
than they can pick and choose which facts are relevant in
determining a physical ailment. Admittedly, the notion of a
fact is a complex one, but this makes it all the more important to exercise care in the use of it. Let us try to appreciate
this complexity in terms of an example.

Someone might think that pushing someone roughly is
rude, and that anyone who denies this is simply refusing to face
the facts. But this example, as it stands, is worthless, since it
tells one nothing of the context in which the pushing took
place. The reference to the context is all important in giving
an account of the action, since not any kind of pushing can
count as rudeness. Consider the following examples:

(a) One man pushing another person violently in order to
save his life.
(b) A doctor pushing his way through a football-match
crowd in response to an urgent appeal.
(c) The general pushing which takes place in a game of
rugby.
(d) A violent push as a customary form of greeting between close friends.

In all these cases, pushing someone else is not rude. If
someone took offence at being pushed, he might well see in
the light of the situation that no offence had been caused.
But what of situations where there is general agreement that
an offence *has* been caused? Is the offence a fact from which
a moral conclusion can be deduced? Clearly not, since what
this suggestion ignores is the fact that *standards already
prevail* in the context in which the offence is recognised. If
one wants to call the offence a fact, one must remember that

it is a fact which already has moral import. The notion of 'offence' is parasitic on the notion of a standard or norm, although these need not be formulated. The person who wishes to say that the offence is a 'pure fact' from which a moral conclusion can be deduced is simply confused. What are the 'pure facts' relating to the pushing and the injury it is supposed to cause? A physiological account of the pushing (which might be regarded as pure enough) would not enable one to say what was going on, any more than a physiological account of the injury would tell us anything about what moral action (if any) is called for as a result. It makes all the difference morally whether the grazed ankle is caused by barging in the line-out or by barging in the bus queue. Any attempt to characterise the fact that an offence has been caused as a non-evaluative fact from which a moral conclusion can be deduced begs the question, since in asserting that a *kind of offence* has been caused, a specific background and the standards inherent in it have already been invoked.

But this does not resolve the disagreement. One might give way on the confusion involved in talk about deducing moral conclusions from 'pure facts', and agree that 'pushing' does not constitute rudeness in all contexts. Nevertheless, one might argue, where the circumstances *are* appropriate, it is possible to determine the rudeness of an action in a way which will settle any disagreement. But, again, this is clearly not the case. Whenever anyone says, 'That action is rude', there is no logical contradiction involved in denying the assertion, since although two people may share a moral concept such as rudeness, they may still differ strongly over its application. This is possible because views about rudeness do not exist *in vacuo*, but are often influenced by *other* moral beliefs. A good example of disagreement over the application of the concept of rudeness can be found in Malcolm's Memoir of Wittgenstein.[1] Wittgenstein had become extremely excited and agitated in a philosophical discussion with Moore, and would

[1] Norman Malcolm, *Ludwig Wittgenstein, A Memoir*, O.U.P., 1968, p. 33.

not allow Moore sufficient time to make his point. Moore thought that Wittgenstein's behaviour was rude, holding that good manners should always prevail, even in philosophical discussion. Wittgenstein, on the other hand, thought Moore's view of the matter absurd: philosophy is a serious business, important enough to justify becoming unmannerly in one's excitement and agitation; to think this rudeness is simply to misapply the judgement. Here, one can see how standards of rudeness have been influenced by wider beliefs; in other words, how the judgement, 'That is rude', is not entailed by the facts. Because of these wider facts people will weigh the facts differently.

The position we have arrived at does not satisfy a great many contemporary moral philosophers. They are not prepared to recognise the possibility of permanent radical moral disagreement. They want to press on towards ultimate agreement, moral finality, call it what you will. They propose to do this by considering certain non-moral concepts of goodness in the belief that they will throw light on the notion of human good and harm. The non-moral example, 'good knife', has often been used for this purpose. The word 'knife' names an object in respect of its function. Furthermore, the function is involved in the meaning of the word, so that if we came across a people who possessed objects which looked exactly like knives, but who never used these objects as we use them, we should refuse to say that they had the concept of a knife. Now when a thing has a function, the main criterion for its goodness will be that it serves that function well. Clearly, then, not anything can count as a good knife. But how does this help our understanding of moral goodness? Moral concepts are not functional. One can see what is to count as a good knife by asking what a knife is *for*, but can one see the point of generosity in the same way? To ask what generosity is *for* is simply to vulgarise the concept; it is like thinking that 'It is more blessed to give than to receive' is some kind of policy.

Yet, although moral concepts are not functional words, they are supposed to resemble them in important respects. The interesting thing, it is claimed, about many non-functional words, is that when they are linked with 'good' they yield criteria of goodness in much the same way as 'good knife' and other functional words do. For example, it seems as if 'good farmer' might yield criteria of goodness in this way. After all, farming is an activity which has a certain point. To call someone a good farmer will be to indicate that he has fulfilled the point of that activity. What 'the point' amounts to can be spelled out in terms of healthy crops and herds, and a good yield from the soil. The philosophical importance of these examples is that they show that the range of words whose meaning provides criteria of goodness extends beyond that of functional words. But what if the range is even wider than these examples suggest? It is clear what the philosophers who ask this question have in mind: what if the meaning of moral concepts could yield criteria of goodness in the same way? If this were possible, one need not rest content with expounding 'good knife' or 'good farmer'; 'good man' awaits elucidation. The goal is to find out what constitutes human flourishing. Furthermore, once these greater aims are achieved, all moral disputes would be, in principle at least, resolvable. Anyone claiming to have a good moral argument would have to justify it by showing its point in terms of human good and harm. And, once again, not anything could count as human good and harm.

The programme is nothing if not ambitious, but the whole enterprise is misconceived almost from the start. As far as land farming is concerned the confusion could have been avoided had one asked why 'farming' yields criteria when joined with 'good'. To say that this type of farming is an activity which has a point, that farming serves some end, and that to call someone a good farmer is to say that he achieves this end, is only to tell part of the story. The most important part is left out, namely, *that the end in question is not in dispute.*[1] That is why it makes sense to talk of experts in farming, and why problems in farming can be solved by technical or scientific means. For example, farmers might disagree over which is the best method of growing good wheat, but there is no disagreement over what is to count as good wheat. On the other hand, the situation is different where animal farming is concerned. Suppose it were established that the milk yield was not affected by keeping the cattle indoors in confined quarters.[2] Many people would say that no good farmer would be prepared to do this, despite the economic factors involved. Others may disagree and see nothing wrong in treating animals in this way. The point to note is that here one has a *moral* dispute. We recognise it as such because of the issues of cruelty, care, and expediency involved in it. The dispute cannot be settled by reference to the point of farming in this instance, since it is agreed that whichever side one takes, the milk yield remains the same. One must recognise that there are different conceptions of what constitutes good farming. Similarly, we shall find that there is no common agreement on what constitutes human good and harm. We shall argue presently that human good is not independent of the moral beliefs people hold, but is determined by them. In short, what must be recognised is that there are different conceptions of human good and harm.

[1] Even this much is true only so long as one equates the point of land farming with productivity. Clearly, however, this is too narrow a conception, since if one is going to speak of 'the point' of farming, far more than productivity is involved.

[2] We owe this example to Dr H. S. Price.

6

The Variety of Morals

The above conclusion would not satisfy the philosophers we have in mind. For them, moral views are founded on facts, the facts concerning human good and harm. We shall argue, on the other hand, that moral viewpoints determine what is and what is not to count as a relevant fact in reaching a moral decision. This philosophical disagreement has important consequences, for if we believe that moral values can be justified by appeal to *the* facts, it is hard to see how one man can reject another man's reasons for his moral beliefs, since these reasons too, presumably, refer to the facts. If, on the other hand, we hold that the notion of factual relevance is parasitic on moral beliefs, it is clear that deadlock in ethics will be a common occurrence, simply because of what some philosophers have unwisely regarded as contingent reasons, namely, the different moral views people hold.

Many philosophers are not convinced that there need be a breakdown in moral argument. It is tempting to think that anyone who has heard *all* the arguments in favour of a moral opinion cannot still ask why he ought to endorse it, any more than anyone who has heard all there is to say about the earth's shape can still ask why he ought to believe that the earth is round. Anyone who has heard *all* the reasons for a moral opinion, has, it seems, heard all the facts. Sometimes the facts are difficult to discern, but there is in principle no reason why moral disagreement should persist. Therefore, it is difficult to see how 'x is good' can be a well founded moral argument when 'x is bad' is said to be equally well founded. So runs the argument.

Certainly, it is difficult for philosophers who argue in this way to account for moral disagreement, since for them, moral judgements are founded on the facts of human good and harm, and the facts are incontrovertible. It is not surprising to find Bentham being praised in this context, since he too alleged that there is a common coinage into which 'rival' moral views could be cashed. The rivalry is only apparent, since the felicific calculus soon discovers the faulty reasoning. On this view, moral opinions are hypotheses whose validity is tested by reference to some common factor which is the sole reason for holding them. Bentham said the common factor was pleasure; nowadays it is called human good and harm. Whether one's moral views are 'valid' depends on whether they lead to human good or harm. But how does one arrive at these facts? One is said to do so by asking the question, 'What is the point?' often enough.

As we saw in Section 3, philosophers are led to argue in this way by misconstruing the implications of the truth that a certain conceptual background is necessary in order for beliefs to have moral significance. Instead of being content to locate the point of such beliefs in their moral goodness, they insist on asking further what the point of *that* is. If one does not give up questioning too soon, one will arrive at the incontrovertible facts of human good and harm which do not invite any further requests for justification. Injury seems to be thought of as one such final halting place. To ask what is the point of calling injury a bad thing is to show that one has not grasped the concept of injury. To say that an action leads to injury is to give *a* reason for avoiding it. Injury may not be an overriding reason for avoiding the action which leads to it, as injustice is, but its being *a* reason is justified because injury is necessarily a bad thing. Even if we grant the distinction between reasons and overriding reasons, which is difficult enough if one asks who is to say which are which, is it clear that injury is always necessarily a bad thing?

The badness of injury, it is argued, is made explicit if one considers what an injury to hands, eyes, or ears, prevents a man from doing and getting; the badness is founded on what all men want. Mrs Foot, for example, expounds the argument as follows,

> . . . the proper use of his limbs is something a man has reason to want if he wants anything.
>
> I do not know what someone who denies this proposition could have in mind. Perhaps he is thinking of changing the facts of human existence, so that merely wishing, or the sound of the voice, will bring the world to heel? More likely he is proposing to bring the circumstances of some individual's existence within the framework of the ordinary world, by supposing for instance that he is a prince whose servants will sow and reap and fetch and carry for him. and so use their hands and eyes in his service that he will not need the use of his.[1]

But, Mrs Foot argues, not even this supposition will do, since the prince cannot foresee that his circumstances will not change. He still has good reason to avoid injury to his hands and eyes, since he may need them some day. One does not need such an extravagant example, however, to find objections to the view that injury is necessarily bad. There are familiar ones close at hand which are far more difficult to deal with than the case of the fortunate prince. For example, consider the following advice, and think of Tolstoy's Father Sergius in the light of it,

> . . . if thine eye offend thee, pluck it out, and cast it from thee: it is better to enter life with one eye, rather than having two eyes to be cast into hell fire.[2]

Or consider how Saint Paul does not think 'the thorn in the flesh' from which he suffered to be a bad thing. At first, he does so regard it, and prays that it be taken away. Later, however, he thanks God for his disability, since it was a

[1] 'Moral Beliefs', pp. 96–7.
[2] Matt. 18, v. 9.

constant reminder to him that he was not sufficient unto himself. Or again, consider how warriors, among whom valour is extremely important, might regard their injuries. Might not their attitude to their injuries be similar to a soldier's attitude to his medals? Another example is worth quoting.[1] Brentano was blind at the end of his life. When friends commiserated with him over the harm that had befallen him, he denied that his loss of sight was a bad thing. He explained that one of his weaknesses had been a tendency to cultivate and concentrate on too many diverse interests. Now, in his blindness, he was able to concentrate on his philosophy in a way which had been impossible for him before. We may not want to argue like Saint Paul or Brentano, but is it true we have no idea what they have in mind?

A readiness to admit that injury might result in incidental gain will not do as an answer to the above argument. True, there would be a gain in being injured if an order went out to put all able-bodied men to the sword, but are we to regard the examples of Saint Paul, the warriors, and Brentano, as being in this category? In some peculiar circumstances where this gain could be foreseen, we might even imagine a person seeking injury rather than trying to avoid it. But is this the way we should account for saints who prayed to be partakers in the sufferings of Christ? Obviously not. It is clear that Paul himself does not regard his ailment as something which happens to be useful in certain circumstances. But in any case, why speak of *incidental* gain in any of these contexts, and why speak of the contexts themselves as *peculiar?* In doing so, is not the thesis that injury is necessarily bad being defended by calling any examples which count against it incidental or peculiar? In so far as moral philosophers argue in this way, they lay themselves open to the serious charge which Sorel has made against them:

> The philosophers always have a certain amount of difficulty in seeing clearly into these ethical problems, because they feel the

[1] We owe it to Mr Rush Rhees.

impossibility of harmonising the ideas which are current at a given time in a class, and yet imagine it to be their duty to reduce everything to a unity. To conceal from themselves the fundamental heterogeneity of all this civilised morality, they have recourse to a great number of subterfuges, sometimes relegating to the rank of exceptions, importations, or survivals, everything which embarrasses them . . .[1]

Is it not the case that we cannot understand Brentano's attitude to his blindness unless we understand the kind of dedication to intellectual enquiry of which he was an example, and the virtues which such dedication demands in the enquirer? Again, we cannot understand Saint Paul's attitude to his ailment unless we understand something of the Hebrew-Christian conception of man's relationship to God, and the notions of insufficiency, dependence, and divine succour, involved in it. These views of personal injury or physical harm cannot be cashed in terms of what all men want. On the contrary, it is the specific contexts concerned, namely, dedication to enquiry and dedication to God, which determine what is to constitute goodness and badness. We can deny this only by elevating one concept of harm as being paradigmatic in much the same way as Bentham elevated one of the internal sentiments. We can say that injury is necessarily bad at the price of favouring one idea of badness.

In so far as philosophers construct a paradigm in their search for 'the unity of the facts of human good and harm', they are not far removed from the so-called scientific rationalists and their talk of proper functions, primary purpose, etc. One of these, in an argument with a Roman Catholic housewife over birth control, stressed the harm which could result from having too many children. He obviously thought that the reference to physical harm clinched the matter. The housewife, on the other hand, stressed the honour a mother has in bringing children into the world. It seems more likely that the scientific rationalist was

[1] Georges Sorel, *Reflections On Violence*, trans. by T. E. Hulme, Collier Books Edn., 1961, pp. 229–230.

blind to what the housewife meant by honour, than that she was blind to what he meant by harm. Are we for that reason to call the honour incidental gain?

How would the scientific rationalist and the housewife reach the agreement which some philosophers seem to think inevitable if all the facts were known? It is hard to see how they could without renouncing what they believe in. Certainly, one cannot regard their respective moral opinions as hypotheses which the facts will either confirm or refute, for what would the evidence be? For the rationalist, the possibility of the mother's death or injury, the economic situation of the family, the provision of good facilities for the children, and so on, would be extremely important. The housewife too agrees about providing the good things of life for children, but believes that one ought to begin by allowing them to enter the world. For her, submission to the will of God, the honour of motherhood, the creation of a new life, and so on, are of the greatest importance. But there is no settling of the issue in terms of some supposed common evidence called human good and harm, since what they differ over is precisely the question of what constitutes human good and harm. The same is true of all fundamental moral disagreements, for example, the disagreement between a pacifist and a militarist. The argument is unlikely to proceed very far before deadlock is reached.

Deadlock in ethics, despite philosophical misgivings which have been voiced, does not entail liberty to argue as one chooses. The rationalist, the housewife, the pacifist, or the militarist, cannot say what they like. Their arguments are rooted in different moral traditions within which there are rules for what can and what cannot be said. Because philosophers believe that moral opinions rest on common evidence, they are forced to locate the cause of moral disagreement in the evidence's complexity: often, experience and imagination are necessary in assessing it. One can imagine someone versed in the views we have been attacking, and sympathetic with them, saying to an opponent in a moral argument, 'If only you could see how wrong you are.

If only you had the experience and the imagination to appreciate the evidence for the goodness of the view I am advocating, evidence, which, unfortunately, is too complex for you to master, you would see that what I want is good for you too, since really, all men want it'. Such appeals to 'the common good' or to 'what all men want' are based on conscious or unconscious deception. It may be admitted that the majority of mothers nowadays want to plan the birth of their children, to fit in with the budget if possible, and regard the rearing of their children as a pause in their careers. But this will not make the slightest difference to the housewife of our previous example. She believes that what the majority wants is a sign of moral decadence, and wants different things. But she does not believe because she wants; she wants because she believes.

The view that there are ways of demonstrating goodness by appeal to evidence which operates *independently* of the various moral opinions people hold is radically mistaken. Sometimes, philosophers seem to suggest that despite the moral differences which separate men, they are really pursuing the same end, namely, what all men want. The notion of what all men want is as artificial as the common evidence which is supposed to support it. There are no theories of goodness.

7

Ethical Relativity

The view which we have presented may be expressed by
saying that moral judgements are to be understood as they
appear within moral practices, and since these practices will
differ under different social conditions, there is no *a priori*
limit to the number of different forms they can take. This
view will be seen by many philosophers as a form of scepticism, comparable perhaps with the relativism of Protagoras.
There are, however, important differences between the view
we are presenting and relativism as traditionally understood, and if our position is not to be misunderstood it will
be necessary to consider in some detail what relativism is
usually taken to be.

Relativism is commonly associated with the name of
Protagoras and his famous statement that man is the measure of all things. Precisely what Protagoras meant by this
statement may be impossible to determine with certainty,
but two interpretations seem plausible. According to the
first interpretation, man is the measure of all things in the
sense that each individual man, just in so far as he holds an
opinion on morality or any other matter, is necessarily correct. Man is the measure of all things, on this interpretation, because each man's opinion is the measure of truth
and goodness. According to the second interpretation,
however, truth and goodness are determined, not by the
opinions of individual men, but by the conventions which
they create. Protagoras seems to have held that although,

taken individually, men are incapable of error, they can sometimes hold opinions which are harmful to others, so that it may be convenient for the majority to form conventions by which these opinions are ruled out as bad or false. Here, the standards of truth and goodness lie not in the opinions of any particular man but in conventions; and yet man remains the measure of all things, for these conventions are nothing but a reflection of what the majority of men have decided to call bad or false.

The first interpretation of Protagoras differs in obvious ways from the view we are presenting, for, in our view, it is not the individual who is the measure of what is morally right or wrong, but rather the individual's judgements on these matters derive their sense from the moral practice to which he belongs. The view we are presenting, however, is less easily distinguishable from the second interpretation of Protagoras. For here, Protagoras too would seem to be maintaining that it is the practice and not the individual which determines what is right or wrong.

In spite of an apparent resemblance, however, we think that there is a fundamental difference between our view and that of Protagoras. This can be brought out by first indicating the part of Protagoras's view which is important and true. Protagoras was right in maintaining that human agreement is a necessary condition for there being concepts of truth and falsity. In this, his view resembles that of Wittgenstein in the *Philosophical Investigations*. Wittgenstein says, 'If language is to be a means of communication there must be agreement not only in definitions but also (queer as this may sound) in judgements'.[1] There would be no concept of colour, for example, and no possibility of making true or false statements about colours, if people did not agree in what they take the colour of objects to be. If a man discovered that his judgements about colour differed repeatedly from those of the majority, he would have to give up making colour judgements. If the majority of people could

[1] Ludwig Wittgenstein, *Philosophical Investigations*, trans. by G. E. M. Anscombe, Blackwell, 1953, I: 242.

never reach agreement in colour judgements, then colour judgements would cease to be made. There is certainly a sense, then, in which it is true to say that the possibility of making true or false colour statements depends on the agreement of the majority.

Nevertheless, although Protagoras was correct in maintaining that the agreement of the majority plays a role in making it possible to have conceptions of truth and falsity, he was wrong in what he took that role to be. On Protagoras's view, the agreement of the majority is not merely a necessary condition for the notions of truth and falsity; it is itself *the measure* of truth and falsity. This is evident from his saying that man is the measure of all things. Man is the measure of truth: whether a particular statement is true is determined by whether the majority say it is true. But this is not Wittgenstein's view. On Wittgenstein's view, we judge the truth of a statement by the criteria for verifying that statement. Whether it is true, for example, that an object is red, will depend on whether that object satisfies the criterion by which an object in given circumstances is judged to be red. If people did not agree in their application of this criterion, it would be meaningless to speak of such a criterion, and meaningless, therefore, to speak of judging whether an object is red. Wittgenstein would have said that people for the most part do not consult the majority before making their judgements, but arrive at the judgements independently of one another. What they assume is that if they arrive at an opinion with sufficient care, those of their fellow men who have taken similar care are likely to agree with it. This agreement is not something they use in order to arrive at a judgement, but something which arises, which shows itself, in the course of making judgements. One does not determine whether a particular object is red by seeing whether the majority agree in thinking it red; until one has judged the colour for oneself one is probably unaware of what colour the majority are likely to think it. But one does assume, if one has judged with care, that the majority of those who have taken similar care will agree with one. This agreement need not hold in all cases. On a particular occasion, there is no absurdity in supposing that a single individual is right and the majority wrong. But agreement with the majority is something one relies on for the most part. If one's judgements about colour turned out to be different from those of the majority one would be thrown into confusion and be unable to use colour concepts.

One may wonder how an agreement which appears only in the course of making judgements may nevertheless be taken for granted before a judgement is made. The answer is that no one makes a judgement in the void but in the course of a social life where judgements are already being made by people with whose ways of thinking one is familiar. Because of this, one can know, without consulting them, what people are likely to think, just as a husband may know, without consulting his wife, what she is likely to think about a particular issue, even though precisely this issue has never arisen before. This is the kind of agreement Wittgenstein is referring to when he speaks of the agreement which is necessary for there to be communication. It is not an agreement which is arrived at by consulting the views of the majority. On the contrary, the character of this agreement is such that it can be taken for granted, and the people who share it do not need to consult one another's opinions. It is the agreement of those who share a form of life. Wittgenstein imagines the objection, 'So you are saying that human agreement decides what is true and what is false', and replies, 'It is what human beings *say* that is true and false; and they agree in the *language* they use. That is not agreement in opinions but in form of life'.[1]

This remark by Wittgenstein may be made clearer by referring again to the two interpretations of Protagoras's statement. It is important to note that these interpretations are not really incompatible with one another. To hold that each man's opinion is necessarily true is not incompatible with supposing that people come together and decide for

---

[1] ibid., I :241.

their own convenience to call some of these opinions, those of the majority, true and others false. On Protagoras's view there would be two spheres: a private sphere of opinions which are necessarily true, and the other a sphere in which for public purposes certain opinions are said to be false, the former sphere being the primary one out of which the latter is built. It would not be an exaggeration to describe the *Philosophical Investigations* as a sustained attack on this kind of view. For Wittgenstein, it is not that people form their opinions in logical privacy and later come together to construct that agreement which he describes as an agreement in form of life. On the contrary, it is the form of life which makes it intelligible to hold particular opinions. One's opinion that an object is red, for example, is the opinion that the word 'red', as it is used, applies to that object. This presupposes that there is already a use of 'red', an agreement in its application, an agreement in the light of which one makes one's particular judgements, and in the absence of which, the notion of judgement would be meaningless.

Moreover, it is important to note in this connection that the agreement to which Wittgenstein refers provides the framework within which can occur not only particular agreements, but also particular disagreements. If two people can reach an agreement on the colour of an object, then equally they can fail to reach an agreement. In either case, it is the general agreement in the application of colour concepts which gives sense to what occurs. A disagreement over whether an object is red, no less than an agreement, derives its sense from a general agreement in the application of the concept 'red'. Without this there would be nothing about which the parties could be said to disagree. Furthermore, there is no reason, on a given occasion, why the majority should not be on the wrong side in a disagreement, why the opinion of a single individual should not be more in conformity with the appropriate criterion than the opinion of the majority at that time. On any particular occasion, the opinion of the majority is not the measure of truth or falsity but *itself needs to be justified* by reference to a generally applied criterion.

This last point is an important one because it brings out very clearly the difference between Protagoras's view and Wittgenstein's. The principle objection to Protagoras's view, and to relativism generally, is that it makes judgements depend on convention in the narrowest sense of that term. For Protagoras, it would seem that a man's opinion about a particular issue ought simply to conform to what the majority of men in his class or society think about that issue. To be right, one must conform, one must follow convention. This suggestion is false for a very obvious reason, namely, that within a moral convention we can distinguish between conventional and non-conventional behaviour. To call all forms of behaviour within a moral convention conventional is to obscure this important distinction. Consider the practice of church-going. People may go to church for all sorts of reasons. Some may go out of superstitious fear, because their parents bring pressure on them to do so, because they enjoy the music and the pageantry, because they want warmth and shelter, because they want to worship God. These different reasons are internally related to the point which church-going will have in the lives of the people concerned.[1] To call these various reasons, which no doubt are but a sample, conventional behaviour is simply to ignore and obscure the immense differences involved. If we try to reduce moral conduct to 'doing the done thing' we fail to account for the differences between them which can be seen to exist.

If someone says that morality is merely conventional, he seems to be suggesting that it involves little of importance. All it comes to is following the crowd or the fashion in which you happen to find yourself involved. This form of moral scepticism, however, cannot account for distinctions which can be drawn between doing the done thing and moral regard. Doing the done thing in this context usually,

[1] Of course, if one wanted to be precise the statement of these matters would have to be more complex to account for mixed motivation.

but not always, involves following prevailing trends, going along with the majority opinion. Where this is so, we can see that the values in question are not adhered to for their own sakes, but only because they happen to be fashionable. A change in fashion would bring about a change in allegiance. Where moral regard is present, however, it may well have to go against prevailing fashions on many occasions. Indeed, the fashions may be regarded as manifestations of moral decadence. Where doing the done thing and moral conduct are equated, however, there can be no talk of the decadence of prevailing fashions. The situation is slightly different where doing the done thing does not involve the majority opinion. What is important in someone's eyes may be to conform to the habits of a certain group, a gang, or a gathering of people who think of themselves as constituting an elite. Even here, however, important distinctions can be drawn between having a regard for values to be found in the group, and simply wanting to belong to the group *no matter what its values are*. In the first instance there might be reason one day to break with the group, perhaps because the group has deserted what it once stood for. In the second instance, this possibility is ruled out.

Whether conventional behaviour is a characteristic of majority or minority groups, the essential difference is in the attitude of the people who so conform as compared with moral regard. Plato brought out some of the most important differences in this context in the *Gorgias* and the *Phaedo*. Only the man who has a regard for moral values develops a feeling for them and an understanding of them. In doing the done thing a person has no understanding of that to which he conforms. This has a counterpart in the world of the arts in the desire to know who the top authors are or what are the hundred best tunes. There is no taste involved, no powers of discrimination. Plato might have said that doing the done thing involves the misunderstanding of thinking that the senses, mere observation, will bring moral understanding. Plato has been criticised for rejecting particular examples of goodness and asking for the essence of goodness. He has been accused of thinking that goodness is simply one thing, and of essence-mongering. He has been accused of being anti-historical in trying to locate goodness in some realm beyond the historical. No doubt there is some truth in these accusations, but what they miss is another reason why Plato thought that goodness could not be understood by mere observation. In his important distinction between popular and philosophical virtue, Plato is saying that moral understanding cannot consist in knowing what people call good. We may know what is called good in our own society and in other societies, but this cannot be equated with a regard for goodness. Plato would have said that to do the done thing is to be servile to one's passions, in this case, the passion for conformity and respectability. Plato points out that this servility may be present even when, on the face of it, moral distinctions are being drawn. A soldier may appear to face death courageously, whereas in fact he dies because he is more afraid of public disgrace than of death. Again, a person may practise self-constraint on a particular occasion simply because he desires a greater pleasure. Plato does not regard these as examples of courage or self-restraint. They are examples of popular virtue, the bartering of pleasures and pains. Socrates says, 'Dear Simmias, I am afraid that if we look to goodness as our standard, this is not the right form of exchange, to barter pleasure for pleasure, pain for pain, and fear for fear, trading the greater for the less, as though they were coins, but the only true currency for which all things should be exchanged is wisdom, and it is only when accompanied by wisdom that courage and self-control and justice—and, in short, goodness itself are really what they claim to be, whether pleasures or fears or all other such things be added or not'.[1] Doing the done thing is an example of popular virtue. The values adhered to are means to further ends. Should they cease to bring those ends, respectability, acceptability, etc., they would be renounced without a backward glance. Of

[1] Plato, *Phaedo*, trans. by W. D. Woodhead, 69 B in *Plato: Socratic Dialogues* ed. Woodhead, Nelson, 1953.

course, there are other reasons why people may conform to moral values on particular occasions. They may do so, not out of a desire to do the done thing, but because the moral rule gives a pseudo-justification of what they want to do in any case. A nominal appeal to values 'authorises' the satisfaction of desire. A good example of what we mean, though taken from another context, can be found in Dostoyevsky's novel *The Brothers Karamazov*. Smerdyakov listens to Ivan's intellectual arguments in favour of atheism and the conclusion that since there is no God, all is permitted. Smerdyakov does not understand the argument. Neither has he worked his way through to Ivan's conclusions in the way Ivan himself has done. All he hears is that all is permitted, and that this can be justified rationally. He uses this fact to rubber-stamp his desire to murder old Fyodor Karamazov. What we have here is not a regard for intellectual values, but an expedient use of them. But in this case, and in that of doing the done thing, Plato would say that although value distinctions are invoked, there is no feeling or regard for those distinctions. We can see with Plato that 'Once these things are separated from wisdom and exchanged the one for the other, the resultant goodness is . . . a mere stage illusion, slavish in reality and devoid of any soundness or truth'.[1]

Right opinion, for Protagoras, ought to agree with the opinion of the majority. We have seen how this notion of agreement distorts what we mean in various contexts by moral regard. It is not the notion of agreement which Wittgenstein has in mind. The agreement to which Wittgenstein refers as agreement in form of life provides for the unconventional as well as the conventional response. It provides for the unconventional response because it may be used on a particular occasion to show that the majority is wrong. Without this general agreement on the application of criteria, the individual, on a particular occasion, really would be at the mercy of the opinion of the majority, for

[1] ibid.

there would be nothing beyond this opinion to which he could appeal. This is why Wittgenstein says that the agreement to which he refers is an agreement, not in opinions, but in form of life. By 'opinions' here Wittgenstein means what any man or group of men would say about an issue at any given time. These are not the measure of truth and falsity, but themselves derive their sense from an agreement in judging which has grown up within a way of life.

We are not suggesting that the logic of colour judgements which we discussed in previous paragraphs is in every respect the same as the logic of moral judgements. Nevertheless, they have this much in common: they depend for their sense on an agreement in form of life. With regard to moral judgements, this point has already been indicated in the first section of this essay. One's condemnation of a particular lie occurs within a way of life in which it is taken for granted that a lie is something to be condemned. The agreement in the way of life forms the background against which the particular judgement has its sense. Without such an agreement it would be impossible, not only to agree with a particular moral opinion, but also to disagree with it. Disagreement in morals, as in everything else, can occur only among people who, sharing a way of life, hold certain things in common which they do not consider to be in dispute. The holding of certain things in common which do not need to be justified or even stated is a necessary condition, not simply for one area of discourse, but for language in general. Language is only possible where one can rely for the most part on people's taking what one says in its intended meaning without one's having to stop and explain constantly what one means. This can occur only where people share what Wittgenstein describes as a form of life of which what we have described as moral practices would form a part.

The error of relativism, as it is traditionally conceived, may be stated in general terms by saying that relativists treat moral judgements as if they were statements about certain of the conditions on which they depend for their sense. Protagoras, having supposed correctly that moral judgements depend on some kind of agreement in judgement, goes on to assume wrongly that moral judgements are statements about that agreement. He assumes that to call something morally right is merely to say that this is what the majority agree to call right, whereas, in fact, an agreement in judgement, though a necessary condition for making a particular moral judgement, is not what the particular judgement itself refers to.

The above conclusions can be underlined by way of illustration. The false assumption we wish to show up is that if a moral judgement is made under certain conditions or against a certain background, what the judgement says, that is, what it is about, must be those conditions and that background. Recognising that people come to have a regard for certain values within an institution or a way of life, people conclude, falsely, that the significance and importance of these values can be reduced to observations about institutions or ways of life.

The above conclusions are based on a confusion between the conditions which make moral values possible and the meaning of the values. For example, it is quite true that if there were no families, the notion of parental obligation or of obligations towards parents would have no meaning. But when a parent fulfils an obligation towards his child or when a child fulfils an obligation towards his parent, they are not saying anything about families. A parent or a child could not develop these feelings of regard except within the institution of the family, but they are not feelings about the institution; they are feelings for the child and the parent respectively. If they were feelings for the institution then one might say that the parent loves his child or the child loves his parent in order to keep the family going! It is interesting to note that one only speaks of striving to keep the family together when the natural family bonds have, for some reason, been disrupted. The life of an institution is at its strongest when the institution as such is not the object of the life within it. Thus, it would seem absurd to say that I read a philosophical work in order to keep a philosophical movement going. It is true, that in the absence of the kind of integrity which philosophical enquiry calls for, a philosophical movement will decline or cease, but this does not mean that the perpetuation of such a movement is the object of one's philosophising. Indeed, in so far as attempts are made to promote philosophy, to advocate it for external reasons, this is a sign that the subject has lost or is in danger of losing its natural impetus, or that its promoters and advocates have not recognised this impetus for what it is. Furthermore, if the perpetuation of an institution or a movement were the reason for adhering to the values which flourish within them, no account could be given of why one should adhere to these values when the institution or movement is in decline or in danger of extinction. For example, one may be in a country where the political regime is committed to destroying the family as an institution. It may be that the regime is succeeding in its aim. It may be a safe prediction to say that future generations will have little or no idea of family life. The chances of the perpetuation of the institution are slim. But would we for this reason say that someone's adherence to the traditional values of the family was pointless? The same is true of adherence to all lost causes. The fact that a cause is lost is not a reason for saying that the values it stood for are worthless. Kierkegaard points out that the death of Jesus would be admirable even if none of the consequences which followed it had taken place. The admirableness of the death does not wait on the outcome. The admirableness of the death is found in the death itself.[1]

Another form which the confusion we are discussing may take is a failure to distinguish between the circumstances which surround a moral judgement and the content of the judgement. For example, it may be true that in being given an upbringing of a certain sort, being taught by certain forceful characters, etc., we come to have a regard for cer-

[1] *Purity of Heart*, p. 121–122.

tain moral values. But this moral regard says nothing about these forceful characters or the way in which we were brought up. Certainly, when we make moral judgements we are not making judgements about these circumstances or telling you anything about them. Furthermore, one can appreciate a man's moral regard without knowing anything about his upbringing or his teachers. Of course, reference to his upbringing may have an explanatory role, for example, in accounting for some of the prejudices he has, but there are no grounds for the suggestion that one can explain a man's moral beliefs in terms of his upbringing or the way he has been taught. Other people who usually know nothing of the circumstances by which a man came to hold his moral opinions can agree or disagree with those opinions. The possibility of this agreement or disagreement between people is not impaired by their ignorance of how a man came to hold his moral opinions. But if the expression of moral opinions were simply a way of expressing the circumstances by which these opinions came to be held, moral agreement or disagreement would be impossible given ignorance of such circumstances. The facts show us that this is clearly not the case.

We have seen that moral judgements cannot be reduced to the conditions or the circumstances in which they are made. It is also clear that in making moral judgements we are not saying anything about the history of the values we invoke. Not only are the circumstances by which the moral agent came to adhere to his moral beliefs, and the conditions in which these beliefs have force and intelligibility, distinct from the content of those beliefs, but the conditions out of which the values developed are also distinct from the meaning of the values.

Many of the general moral judgements we make have probably grown out of more restricted areas of application. There is little doubt that moral ideas bound up with the family influenced wider areas of conduct. One sees a move from 'No one should treat his brother like that' to 'No one should treat anyone like that'. One can note the extension

73

of such ideals as sexual fidelity, care for the weak, and respect for the human person. Ideals held within the family will thus influence conduct outside it. People who hold the former might well extol faithfulness to friends or any contractual agreement one might make, and show strong disapproval of bullying. One could contrast with these values those attitudes which have been influenced by what might be called 'the morality of successful business'. Here the accent will be on enterprise, initiative and expansion. Those who have a regard for these ideals will tend to place less emphasis perhaps on the considerations which those who adhere to a 'family morality' think important. Again, it is fairly easy to see how sport has influenced certain moral ideals. In sport we have the duty to play the game, and various offences are regarded as violating the spirit of the game. These influence wider judgements, as, for example, when we tell someone who takes advantage of a person's generosity, 'You aren't playing the game'. The distinction between what constitutes fairness and unfairness thus becomes part of wider moral attitudes. It is also fairly easy to see how certain military ideals have influenced a wider morality. In the armed forces we find obligations arising from such evaluative ideas as 'give and take', 'share and share alike', 'leader of men', 'team spirit', 'we're all in this together', and so on. But we now say outside such restricted contexts, 'You play your part and I'll play mine'. The morality of the crisis is precisely that of 'give and take' and 'we're all in this together'. If one's moral views have been influenced by these military ideas, one's judgement of character will vary accordingly. Perhaps one may look for the same kind of qualities in men that would be considered exemplary in a military character reference: he mixes well, bears hardship without a grumble, knows how to keep control in awkward situations, is obedient and loyal, and so on. If one were asked whether this man ran after women now and then, one might reply, 'Oh, I don't know about that. What he does with his spare time is his affair. All I know is that he is a good man'. Again, the law-court and the police have their own restricted criteria for judging character. For all practical purposes the question the court wishes to settle is whether the man did that for which he is accused and whether he is likely to give them further trouble. These considerations might influence one's view of people in general. One might be tempted to think of them morally in terms of law-abiding citizens and delinquents. In deliberating over its verdict the court may listen to an employer's testimonial. The testimonial may not draw a sharp distinction between being a good workman and being a good man. Even within family relationships one may identify being a good member of the family with being a good man. But others may say, 'He was good to his family but . . .'. Moral ideas have also been influenced by standards in industry. Although the idea of pride in one's work was present at a far earlier date, work in industry undoubtedly contributed to this idea, or at least, it did fifty years ago. This was extended morally in the ideas of pride and responsibility in an attempted task. The influence of aesthetic judgements on morality can be seen in such expressions as 'noble character', 'beautiful nature', or 'fine deed'.

Along with these various influences, of which we have mentioned just a few, we have the moral teaching delivered on the mother's knee, as it were. This teaching in its turn, of course, may have been influenced by some of the considerations we have mentioned. We do not claim that our account of these influences on moral ideas is historically correct. But, assuming it is, it does not follow that one must have knowledge of it before one can develop a regard for the moral ideals which were so influenced. A man may have a regard for fidelity, fairness, incentive, enterprise, comradeship, endurance, control, the law, respectability, pride in one's work, responsibility, nobility or beauty of character, without knowing the diverse influences which went into the formation of these ideals. It would certainly be confused to reduce the meaning of values to the way they originated or developed. This was Freud's mistake when, after noting correctly that the idea of God as a Father could

not have developed had there not been the institution of the
family in which the concept of a natural father had sense, he
concluded, wrongly, that truths about God could be
equated with truths about our fathers. Once values and
ideals have developed they have a life of their own.

We have given examples of how activities within a restricted context have influenced wider moral judgements.
This serves to underline the fact that such activities and
judgements cannot be understood by assimilating them to
conventions in the narrow sense of that term. The significance of the participation in them is not to be understood in
terms of following the rules of a more or less formal convention. In this respect, the analogy between language and
games which Wittgenstein used for many justifiable reasons
has its limitations. Rush Rhees has pointed out that the
example of the builders which Wittgenstein discusses at the
beginning of the *Investigations* is more like an example of a
game with building blocks than an example of building an
actual house.[1] The actual building of a house is more than a
reaction to certain signals, one man shouting 'Slab!' and
another bringing one. Men go home and discuss their
work with their families, snags crop up in the course of
their work, and so on, but none of these things can be understood simply as reactions to signs. The expressions used by
the builders cannot have their meaning entirely within the
job. We should not be able to grasp the meaning of expressions, see the bearing of one expression on another, appreciate why something can be said here but not there, unless
expressions were connected with contexts other than those
in which we are using them now. Rhees says that when a
child comes to learn the differences between sensible discourse and a jumble of words, this 'is not something you
can teach him by any sort of drill, as you might perhaps
teach him the names of objects. I think he gets it chiefly
from the way in which members of his family speak to him

[1] R. Rhees: 'Wittgenstein's Builders', *Arist. Soc. Proc.*, Vol. LX, 1959–60.
Reprinted in *Ludwig Wittgenstein: The Man and His Philosophy*, ed. by
K. T. Fann, Delta Books, 1967.

and answer him. In this way he gets an idea of how remarks may be connected, and of how what people say to one another makes sense. In any case, it is not like learning the meaning of this or that expression. And although he can go on speaking, this is not like going on with the use of any particular expression or set of expressions, although of course it includes that'.[1]

What Rhees says of the builders can also be said of the examples we have discussed: family life, business, sport, aesthetic appreciation, military life, etc. All these things have bearings on one another, on aspects of human life which are quite intelligible without reference to the activity in question. If there were no such connections, how could moral practices have anything to say about the lives people live? They would be nothing more than games. The internal formalities of such games may be absorbing to the initiates, but they would be a far cry from the importance moral practices have in various ways in the lives people lead. The different games which are played do not make up one big game. Neither do the various activities we mentioned make up one big activity. Nevertheless, the various activities a human being is engaged in do form part of his life. The kind of meaning or unity his life has will depend on the bearing which these different activities have on each other for him. If such bearings are not taken into account, if the activities are thought of as distinct games, cut off from each other, it is not easy to give an account of the difficulties which arise in connection with these activities. Consider the difficulties which a man's relationship to his work may bring into his family relationships in a host of different ways. Or consider how a man's military career may affect the way in which he brings up his son. But if these activities were insulated games one could give no account of such difficulties or influences. One could not see how there could be any difficulties or trials for what one believed, since what one believed would be protected from the

[1] In *Ludwig Wittgenstein: The Man and His Philosophy*, p. 262.

77

possibility of such difficulties and trials in the way in which the rules of bridge, by their very nature, are immune from problems created by the rules of hockey.

Thus we see that to understand human activities and the moral practices they give rise to as conventions in the narrow sense, as games, is to obscure the kind of roles these activities and practices play in human life and by so doing falsify their nature.

8

Moral Dilemmas

In the preceding sections we have sometimes compared value judgements with judgements about colour, and suggested that for certain purposes they may be treated in the same way. There is, however, a danger in this procedure: we may be led to ignore differences between the two kinds of judgement that are greater than the resemblances. In particular, we may fail to see that the relation between a moral principle and a particular moral judgement is very different from the relation between colour criteria and any particular colour judgement. To bring out this difference we need to give special attention to the ways in which moral principles are related to the particular case.

One way in which moral principles differ from the criteria for colour is that the former may conflict with one another. If we hold that it is important not to lie and also important to help our friends, we may find ourselves in a situation where we have to sacrifice one of these principles: the friend can only be helped if we tell a lie. This kind of situation does not arise where colours are concerned. It may be the case, of course, that a particular shade of colour lies on the borderline between two colours, without our being able to assign it clearly to either. But a dispute about the precise colour of this shade, between red and brown let us say, is open to a verbal solution. We may decide to *call* the shade reddish brown. In the case of a moral dilemma, however, there may be no possibility of this kind of compromise. We may simply have to choose between telling the truth and helping our friend, and, whatever our choice, we cannot avoid sacrificing one of our principles.

The recognition that situations of this kind can and do occur has led philosophers to reflect on the nature of moral principles themselves. Such philosophers have argued that moral principles are generalisations which can be expected to hold only for the majority of cases. For example, if we say that truth telling is good, we do not mean that it is good in every conceivable circumstance, but that it is good on the whole. Such qualification is necessary since there are some situations in which a lie may be justified by its beneficial consequences. This is the view which was adopted by the Utilitarians, and has been adopted in our own day by R. M. Hare. On Hare's view, a moral principle is a generalisation which we can expect to modify in the light of experience.[1] Part of what we mean by growth in moral experience is our coming to see that principles which we thought could be applied quite generally admit in fact of a number of exceptions. We may begin by thinking that the principle of truth telling is to be applied in every situation, but, finding that there are situations where that principle admits of exceptions, we modify the principle to allow for them.

This view differs in an obvious way from the one which we set out in the opening section of this work. There we saw that when we justify our moral judgements we make use of such principles as honesty, integrity, truthfulness, etc. These principles are not generalisations which hold in the majority of cases, but rules of ethical grammar; they provide the framework within which particular moral judgements have their intelligibility. These principles are not the subjects of prescriptive judgements. They are what we mean by a justification of such judgements. For Hare, value judgements depend ultimately, not on principles, but on decisions, principles being themselves the products of decisions. This is a view which we have criticised already in

[1] R. M. Hare, *The Language of Morals*, O.U.P. 1952, p. 3.

some detail. We have argued that the need for a decision arises in the light of considerations which are not themselves the product of decisions. In the absence of such considerations, a decision cannot be meaningful. We have urged that phrases like 'Lying is bad' or 'Generosity is good' are not themselves the expressions of moral positions, but an indication of the conditions under which moral positions can be expressed.

There remains, however, a difficulty for the view we are presenting. If one holds that the principle of truth telling has the status of a rule of grammar, forming part of the very conditions under which it is meaningful to call an action good or bad, it may appear all the more difficult to explain why, on some occasions, we might come to the conclusion that a lie is justified. In order to resolve this difficulty we must examine what account should be given of situations where moral principles clash.

When moral principles clash, some philosophers have said that there can only be *one* set of rights and obligations involved. In one sense, they would say, the clash is only apparent, since the rights and obligations which conflict are only presumptive rights and prima facie obligations. They are indications of what tends to be morally required. This way of talking was adopted by W. D. Ross. It is to Ross's credit that, unlike other intuitionists, he tried to give an account of moral dilemmas. Nevertheless, his attempt to do so badly distorts the relation between moral practices and particular decisions in moral dilemmas. For Ross, absolute rights and absolute obligations are those rights and obligations which one ought to satisfy having considered all the prima facie rights and obligations involved. According to Ross, such decisions, to a large extent, are to be reached by an assessment of consequences. We can never be sure, however, of what these consequences are going to be. Hence Ross's remark that there is much truth in the saying that the right act is the fortunate act.[1] For Ross, then, moral dilemmas are practical problems about conflicting tenden-

[1] W. D. Ross, *The Right and The Good*, O.U.P. 1930, p. 31.

cies involving complicated calculation, long-term prediction, and a measure of good luck. This account, however, is a travesty of the nature of moral dilemmas.

Ross's account of moral dilemmas has been criticised by A. I. Melden. Much of what he has to say is a much-needed corrective to Ross. But in relation to moral dilemmas, Melden's criticisms do little to clarify the kind of importance they have. Despite important differences, these dilemmas remain for Melden what they were for Ross: 'mere practical problems'.[1] By bringing out the strengths and weaknesses of Melden's analysis, we hope to throw further light on the relation between moral practices and particular decisions in moral dilemmas.

Melden argues in the main by considering what is involved in giving special consideration to one's parents. He shows that unless one takes into account the status of the father and the relationships between parents and their children which have their life within the institution of the family, one will wonder how the so-called gulf between the matter-of-fact status of being a father and the obligations which children have towards their fathers can ever be bridged. How does the matter-of-fact status of being a father confer any rights on the father? Melden's reply is that if we consider the role a parent plays within the institution of the family we see that 'the right *is* that role".[2]

[1] A. I. Melden, *Rights and Right Conduct*, Basil Blackwell 1959, p. 11.

[2] ibid., p. 84. But this theme runs through the argument of the whole essay.

Melden's use of the notion of a role raises certain objections which do not concern us immediately in this essay. He speaks sometimes as if the role of a father is a role which *any* suitably qualified man can play. If one man fails in the role, another may take over. He ignores the importance of the fact that only one man, in one sense, can be said to be one's father. For a discussion of the moral importance of this natural fact see D. Z. Phillips, 'God and Ought' in *Christian Ethics and Contemporary Philosophy* ed. by I. T. Ramsey, S.C.M. Press 1966, pp. 133–139 and Peter Winch, 'Understanding A Primitive Society' in *The American Philosophical Quarterly* Vol. I 1964, reprinted in *Religion and Understanding* ed. by D. Z. Phillips, Basil Blackwell 1967. See p. 41.

Melden also speaks sometimes as if a description of the parent's role binds

Melden is quite aware that parental rights are not always satisfied, but he does not think, like Ross, that in face of this fact one must say that all parents have are presumptive or prima facie rights. Melden shows very well how one is tempted to say this by thinking that the acknowledgement of rights and obligations entails the fulfilment of those rights and obligations. If this were true, absurd conclusions would follow.[1] First, if it is always obligatory to satisfy moral rights, why do we speak of people demanding, asserting, or standing up for, their rights? The fact that people engage in these activities shows that they recognise that rights compete for satisfaction. But if the satisfaction of moral rights were always obligatory, these activities would be superfluous, amounting to no more than a trivial re-emphasis of the obvious. Second, if the satisfaction of moral rights were always obligatory, it would be self-contradictory to say that one had obligations which one ought not to meet. But we say this in situations which are quite familiar to us. A third consequence would be that if a parent waived his rights, he would be guilty of an immoral action and of encouraging his child to act immorally. But this does not do justice to the ways in which we react to such situations. As Melden says, 'we do not only excuse or pardon parents for waiving their rights, we even praise them for doing so, and not only because of the otherwise commendable love and affection they display towards their offspring but sometimes because of the superior moral wisdom they exhibit'.[2]

For the above reasons, Melden concludes that the recognition of moral rights does not entail that those rights ought always to be satisfied. This being so, there is no necessity for saying that because moral rights compete for satisfaction, the unsatisfied right must simply be a prima facie right. On the contrary, Melden argues, one can only account for the nature of moral dilemmas by recognising that genuine

---

anyone who understands it to a *moral* recognition of parental rights. For a criticism of this see Appendix 1 of this essay.

[1] op. cit., p. 11.   [2] ibid., p. 11.

rights and obligations are in competition. The introduction of prima facie duties obscures the nature of moral perplexity.[1] It does not tell us what it is which gives truth telling, promise keeping, etc. the tendency to be binding which Ross attributes to them. In order to avoid the difficulties which exceptions created for Kant's view of moral rules, one might qualify duties by saying, 'In general one ought to . . .'. But granting that there are exceptional circumstances, the proposed qualification is disastrous. As we have seen already, it makes all moral decisions a matter of probability. We saw this happening in Ross's account of moral dilemmas, and in Hare's view of moral principles as generalisations which we can expect to modify in the light of experience. When we tell the truth, how can we be sure that the case in point is not one of the exceptions? On the other hand, one cannot say that one should always tell the truth when truth telling conflicts with other moral practices. On this view there would be no moral problem concerning truth telling. But quite clearly such problems do arise. There is little point in qualifying the rule by adding, 'except where morally undesirable' since this would reduce it to moral vacuity. It might be thought worthwhile to give a list of exceptions to the rules. Why do we not codify moral rules in much the same way as a teller in a bank is given a list of circumstances in which he is to cash cheques in advance of a certain amount? Melden shows that the mistake is to think that such codification is possible. It is impossible to state the precedence of moral rules in vacuo. The different moral practices do not tell us which takes precedence over the other. This is something we have to decide and learn as we go along. Sometimes, there will be more or less general agreement on the matter. For example, when Herod tells us that he had to execute John the Baptist because he promised Salome anything she asked, few of us would be prepared to accept this as a justification of his actions. Can we then generalise from this example and say that considerations of humanity are always

[1] ibid., p. 21 f.

more important than truthfulness? Hardly. Consider the case of someone who has always promised his mother to tell her when she is dying. He may also know that the knowledge that she is dying will make the end harder for her. Is what he ought to do obvious? Certainly, different people will assess the situation differently. How the son decides, how we might decide, may contribute much to our moral views. What one is able to do in such situations may change one's views on the issues involved, and change one's perspective of such dilemmas when they face other people. We develop as we go along.[1] The individual and the life he lives can bring a great deal to the development of moral understanding. Some of the individual's decisions will have significance for himself alone. At other times, others may be able to learn from them. All this being so, Melden is surely right when he says that 'it is preposterous to suppose that we can so qualify "One ought to tell the truth" that every "exception" can be foreseen and nothing need be left to the good sense of the agent learning how to employ such "rules" '.[2] This can be recognised if we remember Melden's earlier emphasis on the way in which rights and obligations compete for satisfaction. According to Melden, if we keep both these conclusions in mind we can see a way of avoiding Kant's difficulties concerning absolute rules which does not involve treating moral principles as generalisations of probabilities. We are tempted to see certain situations as exceptions to moral rules, for example, the rule that one should give special consideration to one's parents, because we confuse the moral rule as a permanent moral consideration, a reason for doing the appropriate action, with the moral rule's being, if this is the case, a sufficient reason for action. Melden points out that even when parental rights are not satisfied because of overriding moral considerations, what we say is, 'Yes, but . . .' and this is revealing. 'For it does

[1] We are indebted to Mr Rush Rhees for this way of putting the matter. This does not imply that he would approve of everything we have said in this context.

[2] ibid., p. 24.

show that the locution "One should give special consideration to one's parents" is unexceptionable but is not decisive in establishing what is morally required in the given circumstances. Hence the term "exception" is posted on the wrong box. It is one thing to be justified in presenting the wishes of one's parents as a moral consideration, it is another to be justified in claiming on that account that the appropriate action is morally required. Exception may be taken to the latter, but never to the former'.[1]

There is much to applaud in Melden's analysis. In his insistence that conflicting rights and obligations are genuine rights and obligations, not mere presumptive rights and obligations, and his insistence that the values involved in moral dilemmas are absolute in that they can never be subordinated justifiably to non-moral considerations, Melden's account of moral dilemmas is a great advance on that of Ross. Nevertheless, his account does not add a great deal to Ross's with respect to the resolution of moral dilemmas and the agent's attitude towards them. This has consequences for Melden's view of the relation of moral principles to particular moral decisions. Both Ross and Melden stress the practical nature of moral dilemmas. In doing so, they often treat moral problems as if they were technical problems. But there are obvious differences between them. Consider, for example, problems which may arise for a technique like plumbing. These problems are not part of the skill of plumbing. On the contrary, the skill of plumbing is aimed at removing such problems, the principles of plumbing being the means of doing so.[2] Moral principles, on the other hand, are not the means by which moral problems are removed. Moral principles are the source of moral problems, they create them rather than

[1] ibid., p. 44.

[2] The view that moral principles are generalisations to be modified in the light of further experience is probably based on the view that moral principles are similar to technical principles. If a technical principle will not solve one's problem one modifies it, or discards it for one that will. The point is, however, that a moral principle is not a technical principle.

solve them. For example, the reason why a man who has to choose between telling the truth or helping a friend is in a dilemma is that he considers it important to tell the truth and to help a friend. If he could look on either of these as not having moral importance he would no longer be in a dilemma. His dilemma is a direct consequence of holding certain moral principles. One's principles in a technique are the means by which problems are solved, whereas in morality they are the very things which give rise to one's problems.

Again, in a technical problem, the puzzle may be over which of two methods will achieve a desired result. The methods are important in the situation only in so far as they further the problem in hand. In one sense, it does not matter what one does in such contexts. This may not be apparent at first. Surely, one might say, it makes all the difference whether one does one thing rather than another, since if one adopts the wrong method, the desired end will not be achieved. But this is precisely the point we are making. *Any* means would be adopted if they secured the desired end. Thus, once one has determined which of two methods does solve a technical problem, it would be irrational to concern oneself with the other method. Since the result is all important and the means relatively unimportant, once it is shown that a suggested means does not lead to the desired result, the means in question is devoid of importance and not worth bothering about. But moral dilemmas cannot be understood in this way. The 'solution' to a moral problem does not stand to moral principles as the solution to a technical problem stands to the principles of a technical skill. The 'solution' of a moral problem, unlike the solution of a technical problem, cannot be deduced from the principles themselves. Furthermore, the constituents of a moral problem, unlike alternative methods of solving a technical problem, cannot be regarded as means to a further end.

Some philosophers have tried to evade these conclusions by giving one moral principle supreme authority over all others. For example, Utilitarians argue that the greatest happiness of the greatest number is the principle to which all others are subordinate. The right solution to any moral problem may be calculated by reference to this supreme principle. For them, a moral problem is a species of technical problem. What is unclear in Melden's analysis is where he stands on this issue. From the early parts of his essay, one would conclude that he is opposed to Utilitarianism. He seems to be arguing there that there is no one supreme moral principle to which all others are subordinate. What we have is a complex variety of moral principles. This seems to recognise the existence of independent duties, some of which may conflict on a given occasion, so that whichever we choose we may find ourselves having to do what is bad. Later, however, Melden seems to argue differently. He seems to imply that whenever there are conflicting considerations, a man with sufficient insight will always discover that certain considerations have more weight than others and that only one course of action will be right in the circumstances. For him moral dilemmas present 'mere practical problems to be resolved by the moral wisdom of the persons concerned'.[1] As in the case of technical problems, the emphasis is on solving the problem in hand. Speaking of the moral wisdom which he considers necessary in order to accomplish this, Melden says that it 'consists not only in recognising that a right may operate as a consideration that supports the claim that an action is right but also in recognising how to weigh such supporting considerations whenever they compete and how in such cases to arrive at a determination of what it is that one is morally required to do'.[2] Melden says that when a person finds himself faced with conflicting obligations, it would be foolish of him to say that all moral bets are off, as he might say of bets on spinning a coin when the coin lands on its edge. He says that such conflicts are 'familiar incidents in our common moral life which, in the great majority of cases, are easily comprehended by a not uncommon moral wisdom'.[3]

[1] ibid., p. 11.
[2] ibid., pp. 15–16.   [3] ibid., p. 12.

This way of speaking reminds one strongly of the way in which we speak of a skill in some craft. When he speaks about recognising how to weigh supporting considerations he seems to imply that there is some general method by which this skill can be learned. This impression is strengthened by passages in which Melden seems to introduce considerations of a utilitarian kind. Melden argues that even when a person whose rights are not satisfied disagrees with the decision taken, it does not follow that his moral status has been marred. He says that 'What is essential to the determination of the rightness of the given course of action, no less than to the mutual respect that may defy differences about any action, is the maintenance of the moral structure of the relations between all of the parties concerned'.[1] What does Melden mean by 'the maintenance of the moral structure of the relations between all of the parties concerned'? He seems to mean something like this: all the rights and obligations of people involved in a situation are considered, but not all of them are fulfilled or satisfied. Given that the rights and obligations are considered, however, and that a morally responsible decision to act is taken, Melden's suggestion is that the moral relations involved have been maintained. In order to say this, however, one has to assume that the various moral practices, rights and obligations, which enter a situation, form some kind of system or unity in which relations of mutual respect prevail, and where the main aim of all the moral participants is to perpetuate the unity of the system. It seems that Melden has something of the sort in mind when he says that 'to say that a parent has a right to special consideration from his son or daughter is to describe one facet of the complex role that a parent has within the life of a family. Specifically, it is to describe in a very general way, as we have seen, the kind of conduct of the offspring necessary to the maintenance of an aspect of the moral role a parent plays in the life of the family, a role that is essential to the moral community of the family, which in turn is essential to the

[1] ibid., p. 71.

total moral community of which the family is a part'.[1] Where two principles are in conflict, we need not despair of reaching a conclusion because a man with sufficient skill will always be able to resolve the dilemma by discovering which action has the most beneficial consequences, first, for the institution of the family, and, beyond that, for the community as a whole.

It is extremely important not to confuse Melden's argument with orthodox utilitarianism. Melden does not speak of the community, but of the *moral* community, and when he speaks of the family we should remember that this is for him, among other things, a *moral* institution. This emphasis reveals the difference between Melden's views and those of orthodox utilitarianism. The orthodox utilitarian speaks of the interest of the community as something which is to be considered independently of moral principles, which is in fact the measure by which moral principles are to be assessed. On Melden's view, however, we cannot characterise a community properly unless we consider the moral principles which enter into it.

Melden's views can best be explained in terms of an analogy between moral principles and the rules of a game, an analogy which Melden probably derives from Wittgenstein's use of the notion of a game in his *Philosophical Investigations*. In a game, the sense of any particular rule will be derived from the practice of the game as a whole, but if we try to describe the game as a whole, we find that we cannot do it without describing the rules of that game. The presence of any one rule may be justified by reference to other rules, but the rules themselves, taken as a whole, have no justification except that they form a game which gives satisfaction to those who play it. Even this is misleading, however, for if we wish to describe the kind of satisfaction people derive from playing games, all we can do is describe or give examples of games, and this will involve us once more in describing their rules. Melden thinks a similar analysis of moral rules can be given. The sense of any one

[1] ibid., p. 84.

of the moral principles which enter into family life will be derived from the life of the family as a whole, but if we try to describe the life of the family we find that we cannot do it without describing the moral principles that enter into it. Each principle taken separately can be justified in terms of its consequences for the whole, but what constitutes the justification is not something over above these principles when taken together; the justification *is* the way of life in which these principles have an essential part. This may appear utilitarian in that it provides for the justification of any particular principle in terms of its consequences for a common way of life, and for the resolution of any moral dilemma by reference to that end. Where it differs from utilitarianism is that the end in question cannot be described independently of the moral principles when taken together.

Sometimes the analogy between morality and a game may be helpful, but Melden's use of it is very misleading and certainly contrary to Wittgenstein's intentions in introducing the notion of a game. One use Wittgenstein made of the notion was to show that language does not possess the kind of unity which belongs to a logical system. In the *Tractatus* he had thought that if anything is to be a proposition it must have a form which is common to all other propositions. In his later work he rejected this conclusion and argued that there is as little reason for saying that there is a common form to all that we call language as there is for saying that there is a common form to all that we call games. There are resemblances between our different uses of words, but there is no single entity called language of which these different uses are parts, just as there are resemblances between different games but no single entity called 'game' of which the different games are merely aspects. If we apply Wittgenstein's analogy with games to social life generally, we are provided with an argument which tells *against* Melden's analysis, since Melden does wish to speak of society or the community *as a whole*. The analogy with games would suggest that there is no such entity, that the different activities which occur in social life are related to one another, if at all, in only the loosest ways, and are not aspects of a single process.

The point, however, is that the analogy between social life and a game is at best an inadequate one. If we think of the features of a man's life, his life with his family, his work, his membership of a church or of a political organisation, etc. etc., as so many games, we shall find that the analogy can only be taken a little way before it breaks down. The procedures of one game do not interfere with the procedures of another. If a man is playing rugby, he does not have to occupy himself with the procedures of cricket. A man's work, on the other hand, may interfere with his family life or with his membership of various organisations.[1] The various activities of a man's life have a relation to one another which does not hold between games. It is because considerations which belong to different activities in a man's life can affect one another in various ways that one may find oneself confronted by the kind of problem which is described as a moral dilemma.

Melden suggests that when a dilemma involves different moral interests, the moral structure of the community is preserved if these interests are duly considered before the right action is decided upon. This certainly falsifies the possible reactions of people whose moral interests are affected by the resolution of the dilemma. When Melden speaks in this way, he seems to be talking like a chairman at a conference where different interests are represented. All the interests cannot be satisfied on every occasion, but the

[1] There is a comparable reason for saying that Wittgenstein's analogy between language and the notion of a game is inadequate. The different uses of language may not be parts of a single entity, but the relations between them are closer than those between games. Thus the man who plays cricket and rugby is playing different games, and not different aspects of a single game. But different uses of language, say in science and in art, occur within *the same* language and do not constitute different languages.

For a discussion of some of the tensions in the above analogy see Rush Rhees, 'Wittgenstein's Builders'. We have had reason already to draw attention to these tensions in this essay: see Section 7, pp. 76–78.

participants are prepared to put up with this, since their overriding interest is that the conference continues and does not break up. It is extremely misleading, however, to suggest that a parallel exists between this example and the multiplicity of moral practices.

As we saw in the opening section of the essay, moral practices such as truth telling, promise keeping, generosity, etc., are the conditions which make it possible for us to take up specific moral positions on all sorts of questions. We render specific judgements intelligible by appealing to such concepts as honesty, truthfulness, integrity, etc.[1] But this should never be allowed to obscure the fact that people will differ radically in the moral positions they do justify in these terms. Certainly, there is no justification for the assumption that the various positions will have mutual respect for each other. That being so, there is no reason to think that an interested party will be content if his rights are considered, whether or not they are satisfied. The warring moral points of view are not akin to the members of a conference whose main aim is to keep the conference going. The moral points of view do not go to make up 'a total moral community' as Melden seems to think. The values men have a regard for are valued because they are what they are, not because they serve to perpetuate a so-called total moral community. Melden's attempt to include different moral points of view within some kind of communal unity is as fruitless as Philippa Foot's attempt to base people's moral views on one common factor, namely, human good and harm.[2] Just as the views of the rationalist, the Roman Catholic housewife, the pacifist and the militarist which we considered at the end of the sixth section of the essay, could not be shown to be based on a common conception of human good and harm, so they cannot be shown either to form anything like Melden's total moral community. When the values of opposing points of view are satisfied at the expense of one's own, one will not say necessarily that a right action has been performed. For Melden, 'To be right is the very same thing as

[1] See Section 1, p. 9 f.   [2] See Sections 5 and 6.

to be the kind of action that does serve, however that may
be, the moral community'.[1] But since doubt has been cast,
with good reason, on Melden's conception of a total moral
community, equal doubt can be cast on his notion of what
constitutes a right action. No doubt Melden has given an
account of one moral attitude to other moral points of view.
What he has no right to do is to present that attitude as if it
were a conceptual analysis of the very notion of right action.

Since different moral practices do not make up a total
moral community, the presence of many such practices in a
given individual's life may occasion situations which are
moral tragedies, where, whatever he does, he is going to
hurt someone he loves. When as a result of his action, that
harm comes about, he will not be able to console himself
with the thought that moral wisdom has triumphed, or that
the perpetuation of a total moral community has been
served. He will be faced with the fact that he had to do
what he did. It is absurd to suggest that whenever a
dilemma of this kind occurs a solution can always be found
by considering the consequences which the alternative
actions would have on the moral structure of the community. Leaving aside the difficulties we have noted about this
idea, and even supposing that a solution of this kind could
always be found, it would still be applied only at the cost of
sacrificing something of importance. Suppose, for example,
that a man has to choose between his work and his family,
and suppose it could be demonstrated that one of these
alternatives, say, leaving his family, is clearly the right one.
It still would not follow that leaving his family has now
become a matter of indifference to him, or that his decision,
though it is the right one, is something in which he can
rejoice.

In this respect a moral dilemma is different from anything that will arise as part of a game. The elements which
comprise a moral dilemma, the principles involved in it, are
significant in themselves, whereas the rules of a game do
not have this kind of significance. In rugby football, for

[1] op. cit., p. 71.

example, the rule preventing wing forwards from leaving the scrum before the ball has emerged was introduced because wing forwards had been leaving the scrum quickly and by so doing preventing the development of handling movements. The introduction of this rule was therefore purely utilitarian, having as its object the preservation of a certain character in the game. One could easily imagine the rule being abolished and the earlier practice reintroduced if for some reason half-backs and three-quarters began to dominate play unfairly. In either case, there would be no difficulty, because the rule is of no importance in itself. These remarks apply even to as fundamental a rule of rugby as that one should aim to carry the ball over one's opponent's line. Even this principle has significance, not in itself, but because, when taken with other rules, it forms a game which people enjoy to play.

The significance that we attribute to a moral principle is of quite a different kind. The feeling that one owes to one's father what one could never owe to a stranger is not aimed at preserving the character of the family, nor was this principle introduced at a certain time by a person or persons having in mind a particular end. It is true that the principle has arisen and has its sense within a particular way of life. It is the life of the family and the place of the parent within that life which gives significance to the principle that a parent has a right to special consideration. But in saying this we are saying nothing about the kind of significance the principle has. Certainly, we are not saying that the significance of the principle lies in its consequences, in its utility in preserving the special character of the family. Someone who has experienced the life of the family and the place of the father within that life will feel that he owes his father what he could never owe to a stranger. He does not feel in this way because he wishes the family to be preserved; he merely feels in this way, and considerations about preserving the life of the family do not enter his head. Given that the principle has arisen, it has a significance of its own which is not to be explained in terms of its consequences. A man may regret having to go against this principle however justified he may think himself in doing so.

The view that the principles which arise in the life of the family are not directed towards preserving that life, that the life of the family is not the product of design, may be applied to social life more generally. Generally speaking, human institutions are not the product of design, though they are the result of human actions.[1] An economic system, for example, is sustained by, among other things, the actions of individual business men, but the business men are concerned, not with sustaining the economic system, but with securing their own profit. Each business man is concerned with the economic system only to the extent that it affects his own business, and none has a view of the system as a whole. The total order which emerges as a result of their actions is therefore not the product of their design. Though the characters of the two activities are different, remarks of a similar kind will apply also to literary activity. Where writers are producing good work, literature will flourish. This flourishing will have wider social effects, but the writer is not concerned with making literature flourish, nor with the effect of literature on society, but with the particular work that is before him.[2] Those institutions or activities will flourish which are sustained by spontaneous actions, and it is normally where an institution is in decline that conscious effort is needed to sustain it.[3] The life of the family will flourish where the respect of the child for his

---

[1] See F. A. Hayek, *Studies in Philosophy, Politics and Economics*, Chap. 6.

[2] 'An artist writes a book, paints a picture—I mean when he does so in earnest—not to 'solve the social question' but because, in the first place, he cannot do otherwise and because, in the second place, he will then no longer have it to do'—Jacques Rivière.

[3] It is worth remarking that such an effort is unsuccessful more often than not. 'Restoring art that has lost its unattainable aim is like attempting by reason to restore the youth of a religion. The source can be affected only by a fresh source, and not by any of its own issues; and, in fact no religion that has once died has experienced resurrection, and no art that has once declined has ever been renewed from within. Art cannot save art; and still less when artists have failed can critics save it'—A. R. Orage.

parents, or the affection of the parents for the child, arises naturally and spontaneously, where the principles which one finds in this form of life are not mere instruments for preserving a particular form of existence, but are thought to be important in themselves.

Melden's analysis of moral dilemmas conflicts with the points we have made in the above paragraphs. His view is that conflicting obligations are not instances of tragedy, but are comprehended in the majority of cases by a not uncommon moral wisdom. We do not know how Melden knows that an easy moral comprehension is to be found in the majority of cases. What Melden says does apply to very many cases. For example, if a person's father is taken ill suddenly, and he has promised to go out with his friends, what he ought to do is obvious. We could multiply cases where what one ought to do is a matter of easy comprehension. In these cases, the way ahead is obvious. But are these the kinds of examples we think of when we discuss serious moral dilemmas? We suggest not. That Melden should take such examples almost as a paradigm of moral dilemmas is due to his assumption that a moral dilemma is a kind of technical problem, the kind which might arise in plumbing or in the course of a game. For him, a moral dilemma, as we have seen, is a matter of balancing different elements with the object of maintaining a certain order. The elements themselves cease to be important once they have been successfully balanced. Thus, there will be no cause for tragedy if, in order to attain the balance, some of the elements have to be sacrificed. What is important is that a solution has been reached: things have been kept going. It would be foolish in the above example for the person involved to worry over his broken promise to his friends. Melden might say it was irrational of him to do so. But serious moral dilemmas are not matters of easy comprehension. It is misleading to say, as Melden does, that 'Conflicting obligations are not instances of tragedy',[1] since sometimes, that is precisely what they are. Why does Melden say that in face of

[1] op. cit., p. 12.

conflicting obligations, 'It will not do to say that in such cases all moral bets are off on the ground that if he is morally damned if he does and morally damned if he does not, he is enmeshed in tragedy and deserves not censure but under-standing and sympathy'?[1] The answer is to be found again in his thinking that moral dilemmas are akin to technical problems. In the latter, as we saw, the constituents of the problem are relatively unimportant, the end sought all important. In a moral dilemma, on the other hand, the constituents of the problem are important in themselves, not as means to some further end. In a technical problem, it is possible to give an account of what one is trying to attain, without referring to the possible methods of attaining it. In a moral dilemma, however, the constituent rights and obligations are the objects of our care and concern. We cannot give an account of the moral dilemma without referring to its constituents. When a technical problem is resolved it would be foolish to worry over the discarded method. But in moral dilemmas, since it is the conflicting rights and obligations we are worried about, it is not sur-prising to find the person involved still caring about the unsatisfied right and the unfulfilled obligation. Philosophers have thought such care irrational because they have con-fused moral dilemmas with technical problems.

Consider some remarks by Wittgenstein concerning the dilemma facing a man who has come to the conclusion that he must either leave his wife or abandon his work of cancer research: 'It may be that he has a deep love for her. And yet he may think that if he were to give up his work he would be no husband for her. That is his life, and if he gives that up he will drag her down. Here we may say that we have all the materials of a tragedy; and we could only say: "Well, God help you" '.[2] Melden's analysis of moral dilemmas obscures the moral importance of situations such as these. This is due, to a large extent, to its abstracting the

[1] ibid., p. 12.
[2] Rush Rhees, 'Some Developments in Wittgenstein's View of Ethics' in *The Philosophical Review* Vol. 74, 1965, pp. 22–3.

progress to be made as the sole matter of importance in a moral dilemma. The descriptions which Melden gives of situations where obligations clash betrays this emphasis. For example, he says that 'To favour one's parent in this or that situation *may* entail a needless sacrifice of the development of one's own talents'.[1] Let us enlarge on this remark by giving it a possible context, one which will bring out the limitations in Melden's account of moral dilemmas.[2]

A possessive mother opposes her son's plans to accept promotion in his work, promotion which would develop his obvious talents, but which would involve his living away from home in another part of the country. The son is in no doubt that his mother's possessiveness is mistaken, but he does not want to hurt her. She has sacrificed and suffered much for his sake. He knows that if he moves she will go to pieces. He also realizes that if he turns the promotion down his life will seem empty and that this in turn will destroy his relationship with his mother. He asks himself what he ought to do. Eventually, he decides to accept the promotion, but he still feels remorse for what he has done to his mother. 'Remorse' is a word which does not feature very prominently in Melden's essay. To use Melden's language, whatever the son decides, it cannot serve the moral status of all the persons affected. The son is faced not only with obligations towards his mother who has done so much for him, but also with obligations towards those in his work who have developed his talents and have provided a further opportunity for their development. If we think of the dilemma as a mere practical problem, then once the son has decided to accept promotion, having considered the mother's rights, we might say that the situation has been furthered by a not uncommon moral comprehension. If the mother's rights have been considered, and have been found to be insufficient grounds for action, then that is that. To

[1] op. cit., p. 10.
[2] For a parallel analysis of a similar example see D. Z. Phillips and H. S. Price, 'Remorse Without Repudiation' in *Analysis* Vol. 28, No. 1, 1967. We are grateful to Dr Price for permission to use the analysis in this essay.

feel remorse for not satisfying her rights in this context, it may be said, is as irrational as worrying over a technique which does not achieve the desired result. If a man travelling to London comes upon cross-roads, he will be faced with the choice of which of the roads to take. The roads between which he has to choose, however, have no intrinsic importance. He might, of course, acquire a preference for one of the roads because it is more pleasant to travel along, but this is a matter of taste and has nothing to do with his technical problem. Considered as a technical matter any road will be the right one provided that it takes him to London. So if road A is the right one, he will simply be foolish to regret that he is not travelling along road B. But the problem is entirely different in the example we have been considering. He cannot say that his concern is simply with the solution of his problem and not with considering his mother and his work, in themselves. If he has no concern with his mother and his work in themselves he has no moral problem. His problem just *is* deciding what to do when he is concerned both to consider his mother and his work and finds that he cannot do both.

Moreover, since the character of the problems are different, what constitutes irrationality will not be the same in the two cases. If a man wishes to go to London and will get there by taking road A, then, in the absence of other considerations, he is merely irrational in wishing to travel along road B. But the man who considers it right to consider his work and yet still feels remorse for neglecting his mother is not being irrational. Of course, if a person later came to think that he had taken the wrong decision, he could feel remorse for the harm he has caused his mother. But this is not the situation we have in mind. We are suggesting that even when a person has not had second thoughts, even when he would act in exactly the same way if he had his time over again, he could still feel remorse for harming his mother. Many philosophers find it hard to account for this possibility because they argue that a person can only feel remorse when he has done something he ought not to have done, when he repudiates the action for which he now feels remorse. But this view of moral dilemmas is too narrow. What does the presence of remorse mean in the absence of any repudiation of the action which leads to it? We suggest it is a mark of the seriousness with which he takes the dilemma. Consider the difference between a man who feels regret for harming his mother, and a man who feels remorse because of it. The man who feels regret about harming his mother might speak like this: 'The last thing I wanted to do was to hurt the old lady, but it was unavoidable. She brought it on herself. These things happen, and we have to make the best of them'. The man who feels remorse cares deeply because he, a son, has harmed his mother. He is not blind to the extent to which his mother has brought the situation on herself, but, nevertheless, he feels shame and sorrow for the harm he has caused her and feels responsible for it in a way in which the man who feels mere regret does not. His mother's rights are not, for him, mere objects of consideration which can be forgotten once it has been shown that they are insufficient grounds for action. They are objects of his love and care. As such, they can occasion remorse even when the action which occasioned the remorse is not repudiated. One may, perhaps, say that he should not consider these things as important in themselves, but this is to say that he should not have had the problem in the first place. Given the character of his problem, it is merely a misunderstanding to suppose that he would be irrational in feeling remorse. It is to suppose that the man is confronted by a technical problem when really he is involved in a moral dilemma.

Moral insight into the possibility of remorse without repudiation may well go hand in hand with other insights. It helps one to understand how people can feel an obligation to help others, and show compassion and pity, whether questions of rights are involved or not. These moral insights are connected with seeing that very often there is no clear choice between good and evil. Striving for decency does involve one in evil, but its purpose is to lessen the evil.

It is not possible to contract out of such striving for fear of what one might become as a result. Certainly, such fear seems a far call from Melden's view of moral dilemmas as 'familiar incidents in our common moral life which, in the great majority of cases, are easily comprehended by a not uncommon moral wisdom'.[1]

As we have seen, the various activities of a man's life have a relation to one another, and may interfere with one another in such a way that they pose conflicting obligations for him which cannot all be satisfied. A person can be faced with a situation where, whatever he does, he is going to hurt someone. In such a situation he may arrive at the realisation that even when the right thing has been done there may still be reason for remorse.

The argument of this section may be summarised in the following way. Though moral judgements, like judgements in a technique or judgements about colours, depend for their sense on common criteria, the relation between the criteria and a particular judgement is often different from anything to be found in the other cases. If a man is confronted by a choice between telling the truth and helping a friend, the sense of his problem depends on there being principles which he has derived, independently of his own decision, from the society in which he lives. Unless a man thought, independently of his own decision, that it was good to tell the truth and good to help a friend, he would not have the moral problem of choosing between them. Nevertheless, though the man's problem is derived from these principles, the solution to his problem, the decision he eventually makes, cannot be so derived. This follows from what has been said. It is just because the moral dilemma consists in a conflict between principles that the principles themselves can provide no solution to the dilemma; nor is there any *a priori* reason why there should be any other principle which will provide such a solution. It is because Melden fails to recognise this point that he is open to criticism.

[1] op. cit., p. 12.

Moral dilemmas very frequently are what Melden says they are not, namely, cases of tragedy where a man feels he will be doing evil whichever course he adopts. Of course, there will be occasions where an apparently hopeless dilemma is resolved because, having looked more closely at the particular circumstances, one discovers a further alternative which had been overlooked. At other times, even though no such alternative is present, some of the considerations may, for the person involved, so outweigh the others that he is in little doubt about which is the right course to take. Even in this latter case, however, the man may dislike what he feels it right to do. The course which seems right to him need not appear so to another, even though the other person may share his principles. In cases of this kind everything depends on the weight which is given to the principles involved. There is no general method by which principles are weighed. Two men may share a respect for truth and generosity, but one might place greater weight on generosity and the other place greater weight on truth. Therefore, on particular occasions, though sharing the same principles, they might arrive at different decisions. The difference between such decisions is not likely to be resolved by argument.

These latter remarks raise questions about the precise nature of the disagreement which arises in cases of this kind. The discussion of this question, however, will be postponed until more attention has been given to the nature of moral disagreement, a topic which requires a section to itself.

9

Moral Disagreement

As we have seen in this essay, one cannot deny the multiplicity of moral practices to be found within our society and as between different societies. Any attempt to explain away, or impose a unity on, this heterogeneity in morals simply leads to a distortion and falsification of the facts. But why should such attempts be made? One reason is that some people seem to think that if we admit that there are different conceptions of good and evil, we can never really know what is good or evil. If people differ over what is right and wrong, many feel that we can never really know what is right and wrong. We have seen in this essay how, within our own society, given the same facts, there can be moral disagreement about them. We have seen too that the possibility of moral deadlock seems to shock many contemporary moral philosophers.[1] They seem to think that if there cannot be agreement on an issue, we cannot really know whether it is right or wrong, good or evil. Surely, they argue, every rational person wants to know what is right. We want to know which, if any, among these alternative moral positions is the correct one.

The difficulty, however, is to know what these requests mean. One understands what is meant if someone asks which of two astronomical theories about a star is the correct one. But what does one want to know in asking which morality is the correct one? In the case of conflicting

[1] For further examples see Appendices 2 and 3.

theories about the star, we can imagine, roughly, the sort of empirical evidence which might settle the dispute. But there is nothing comparable in morality. There is something independent of the astronomical theories against which their validity can be checked, namely, the star in question. But moral practices are not theories. They are not accounts or interpretations of anything more ultimate than themselves. This does not mean that the notion of the independently real has no place here. On the contrary, its place is within the moral practice. The individuals who participate in such practices cannot say what they like. Their moral status is determined in the light of their relation to the ideals and duties of the moral practices. What is essential to recognise is that the moral practices are the means not the object of assessment in this context. Consider, for example, a moral disagreement over the way in which prisoners of war ought to be dealt with. A captured warrior may demand the right to die with his sword in his hand. We might say that we know better. The correct thing to do is to prepare him for rehabilitation when aggression ceases. Here we have a direct clash between what might be called a heroic morality and a welfare conception of human life. If one said to the warrior, 'We'll take you to a rehabilitation centre', he might reply, 'Don't treat me like a woman!' In the event of a discussion, the adherent to the welfare conception might make a final appeal to the 'truth' that all men want to live, to which the warrior might reply, 'Not at the cost of sacrificing dignity and valour'. Here one has rival conceptions of human dignity. But when deadlock is reached, that is that. It is this admission which inspires philosophical protests. Moral seriousness, it is said, demands that we press on to a resolution of the disagreement. Nothing less than moral finality must be our objective. Despite the clash of values we must go on to ask which values are the right ones. But what does this question amount to?

If we are one of the parties involved in a moral disagreement, it is queer for us to ask, having taken our stand,

105

'And who is right?' If we do ask this question it is an indication of doubt on our part. We may be impressed by the strength of our opponent's convictions, and in that way be led to review the issue. On the other hand, if we are sure about our moral convictions what further questions about rightness remains? If we were asked why we are right, our answer would be in terms of the content of the moral values involved. Certainly, we would not say that our rightness consisted in our saying that we are right. The reasons we give for saying that a certain course of action is right will have no reference to ourselves at all.

The objection to this way of talking seems to be that we are in no better a position than our opponent to say who is right on any moral question. But what does this reference to a better position amount to? If one man in a theatre has an unimpeded view of the stage, and another man is sitting behind a pillar, we know what it means to say that the first man has a better position in the theatre than the second. We also know what it would mean to say that the first man is in no better a position than the second. He might have been sitting behind a pillar as well. But when philosophers say that one is in no better a position than anyone else to say what is right and what is wrong, they are not saying that *as a matter of fact* one is not in a better position than anyone else. If they were saying this, there might be no objection to their remarks. It may be true sometimes that we are in no better a position than anyone else to judge the rights and wrongs of a complex situation. 'Judgement must be left to God' we might say. At other times, it need not be like this. A father may be in a better position to see that what his daughter takes to be love is in fact something else. In other words, we know what it means in familiar moral contexts to speak of being in a better position and not being in a better position than others to make a moral judgement. But this is not the point that the philosophers are making. When they say that one is in no better a position than anyone else to say what is right or wrong, they mean that one can *never logically* be in such a position. One is tempted to ask, in that case, what it is that one can never be in. They want to say that one is not in a better position, but cannot say what being in a better position would amount to.

If we object to talk about 'being in a better position' to assess which morality is the correct one, this is not because, as a matter of fact, no one has been in such a position, but because the very notion of 'better position' in this context is meaningless. This way of talking is confused. The confusion involved brings us back to the suggestion that moral values must be checked by reference to something beyond themselves. But if we and our opponents appeal to conflicting values in a moral disagreement, these values are not imperfect expressions of something else. These *are* the values we think important, worth defending, and fighting for. This does not mean that we and our opponents are right from our different points of view. Who says that? Certainly not our opponents or ourselves. For example, we may disagree with them strongly about abortion. They may place great emphasis on the choice, circumstances and attitude of the woman expecting the child. We may place equal emphasis on the fact that a child's life is at stake. Each party may be distressed about the other's attitude and condemn it. The respective values adhered to by the people involved in the disagreement determine their attitudes to abortion. Would it mean anything to say that their respective moral positions are only *their* point of view? It might serve as a reminder to someone that there are moral points of view other than his own. But otherwise the remark is idle. What moral values could one have which were not one's own? The fact that one has a moral point of view is not a limitation or a sign of prejudice, but a minimal condition of seriousness concerning moral questions.

Some philosophers, in an attempt to avoid the partiality which they seem to think is involved in the existence of different moral opinions, appealed to the views of a disinterested observer. Where there are a number of conflicting moral assessments of a situation, the right assessment of it is supposed to be the way the situation appears to such an observer. Sometimes it is true that people get so bound up in difficult situations that they cannot see clearly the moral issues involved. At such times, someone with moral insight who is not directly involved, may be able to draw their attention to the moral issues. But this is not the role of the disinterested observer. He is supposed to be able to tell us what the right moral beliefs and decisions are. But how is this supposed to work? Consider moral disagreements about abortion. Has the answer of the disinterested observer any relation whatever to the kinds of issues raised by abortion? In other words, is his answer a moral answer at all? If not, it is difficult to see how a non-moral answer can settle a moral issue. On the other hand, if the observer's answer is a moral answer, it has to do battle with all the other moral attitudes concerned. It enjoys no privileged metaphysical status.

A recognition of the multiplicity of moral practices should not lead to moral scepticism. On the contrary, one can distinguish between this variety where, in different ways and forms, concern is shown for moral considerations, with expediency and a complete lack of concern for any moral considerations. Furthermore, nothing we have said precludes the possibility of discussion between adherents to different moral views. This is because the facts are more complex than we have suggested in this section. We suspect that very many people have no such thing as a complete moral code, a systematic morality. More often than not our lives are affected by diverse moral influences. We feel the attraction of different moral views, and may be torn between them. Furthermore, many moral viewpoints develop in relation to one another; there is the thrust and counter-thrust of moral warfare, so to speak. In order to hold a moral viewpoint, to understand it, expound it and defend it, it may be necessary to take account of the moral viewpoints of one's opponents. On the other hand, we should not be afraid to say that we fail to get the feel of a moral problem because it is part of a moral viewpoint so disparate from our own that we fail to find a conceptual foothold which would enable us to understand it.

The last point above has particular relevance to the consideration of moral practices in cultures other than our own. We are often far too ready to say that actions which are prohibited in one culture are condoned in another. Before we can make this judgement, however, we must be sure that we are referring to *the same* actions. This caution is necessary because of the tendency to impose a description on actions in other societies which assumes that those actions have the same significance there as they would have in our own society. Consider, for example, the practice of child-sacrifice in pre-Abrahamic Hebrew society. Now suppose someone says that God told him in a dream to sacrifice his son. We would not accept this, no matter what he says. We might say that to ascribe such a command to God is impossible. To this, it might be replied, 'If God asked someone to sacrifice his son once, why shouldn't He do so again?' The fallacy in this reply, however, is the assumption that God would be asking our contemporary to do *the same* thing as He asked Abraham to do. What Abraham was asked to do can only be understood by reference to the complex social institutions in which the act has meaning. One would have to take account of the tribal cult, Abraham's status in the tribe, the religious character of the family, and, above all, the practice of child sacrifice. It is logically impossible for us to repeat Abraham's action. Even if we followed his exact route to Mount Moriah, bound our sons to the altar, raised the knives, we should not be doing what Abraham did. We can no more repeat Abraham's action than we can take the advice of the *Daily Express* on the accession of Elizabeth II to the throne and make this another Elizabethan age.

It might be thought, however, that Abraham's remoteness in time makes the problem of moral disagreement an unreal one. After all, we do not have to make up our minds about Abraham, and the likelihood of our next-door neighbour's wanting to sacrifice his son is not great. But what if we are in a position where something has to be done? We may be members of the advance party of an industrial firm involved in exploring a remote area. Suppose that we come across a group of people around an altar about to kill a baby. Or suppose that we come across a group of warriors inflicting wounds on a prisoner. What are we to do? No doubt, as a first move, we shall try to stop the killing and infliction of wounds taking place. That does not mean, however, that we understand what is going on. On the contrary, our intervention is partly due to a desire to be sure about what is going on. If one lived with the tribes in question one might or might not revise one's judgement. It may be the case that they were attempting to murder the child and to torture the prisoner for pleasure. But this may not be the case. One may come to see that these people were no more murdering the child than Abraham was attempting to murder Isaac. The killing of the child is a religious sacrifice. One cannot identify it with murder if only because the people concerned have a notion of murder. To call child sacrifice murder would be to obscure the moral and religious values of the people in question. To see that killing the child was sacrifice and not murder does not mean that one condones the action. It may mean that one no longer thinks it proper to intervene to stop the sacrifice taking place. On the other hand, one might still want to *call* the sacrifice murder. In that case, however, one would have to distinguish carefully between the different uses of the word. What is certain is that one cannot view the situation as one did before one discovered its significance; one cannot say without further ado that a murder is being committed. Similar observations may be made about our other example. We may come to see that the infliction of wounds is not torture, but the according of a warrior's tribute to the prisoner, giving him the opportunity to show the bravery with which he can endure suffering. Having discovered this we may not feel that we ought to interfere. Some people may still want to condemn the practice, but they cannot equate it with what would constitute torture in our society. *That* concept of torture may be found among the warriors too. The temptation to be resisted is the desire to say of our examples that *really* murder is being committed and torture inflicted no matter what the people concerned might say. This is the temptation of thinking that actions in other cultures which look similar to those in our own *must* have the same significance.

Our point is not to deny the possibility of adverse moral judgements on moral practices in cultures other than our own when those practices have been understood. What we are insisting on is that our judgements of these practices must wait on an understanding of them. Whatever our judgements are, they must not distort the nature of the actions judged by ignoring the cultural institutions within which they have their meaning or the relations of ideas involved in the participants' understanding and execution of them.

Whether we are considering moral practices within our own society or moral practices within other cultures, we shall not be tempted to reduce them to an artificial unity if sufficient attention is paid to the ways in which moral opinions and moral values determine our assessments of problems and situations. Iris Murdoch, after quoting Wittgenstein's remark that 'What has to be accepted, the given, is—so one could say—*forms of life*' comments, 'For purposes of analysis moral philosophers should remain at the level of the differences, taking the moral forms of life as given, and not try to *get behind them* to a single form'.[1] Because contemporary moral philosophers do seem to want to reduce moral practices to a single form, whether that single form be thought of in terms of human good and harm or in terms of a total moral community, they obscure the kind of importance moral practices often have in people's lives. In this essay we have tried to give some examples of the contributions which moral practices make to human action and reflection. The examples we have used

[1] Iris Murdoch, 'Vision and Choice in Morality', *Arist. Soc. Proc.*, Supp. Vol. XXX, pp. 40–1. Reprinted in *Christian Ethics and Contemporary Philosophy* ed. by I. T. Ramsey, S.C.M. Press 1966.

have been diverse. We present them, however, not with a view to presenting any unified positive theory of human nature. On the contrary, we agree with a contemporary philosopher when he says that 'The variety is important—not in order to fix your gaze on the unadulterated form, but to keep you from looking for it.'[1]

[1] Rush Rhees, op. cit., p. 25.

Melden's Discussion of the Notion 'Father'

It will be of some interest to compare the remarks which are made in the opening section about the relation between fact and value with the remarks which A. I. Melden makes about the concept of a father in *Rights and Right Conduct*. Melden argues that it would be a mistake even to ask for a purely factual equivalent for the concept of a father, since this concept is to be understood as it occurs within the complex 'institution' of the family, and within this institution the father plays a 'role' which carries with it certain rights and obligations.[1] To understand the role of a father within the institution of the family is to understand that he is a person who has a right to special consideration. The relation between a father and a son, for example, is more than a merely biological one; it is at least partly to be understood in terms of the rights and obligations which each acknowledges with regard to the other. But equally these rights and obligations themselves are to be understood in terms of the roles which father and son play within a complex institution, so that in the notion of a father, or that of a son, we have a concept in which factual and evaluative elements are inextricably mingled.

There is a sense in which Melden seems to us correct in the account he gives of the concept 'father'. What is not

[1] See p. 84.

clear, however, is the precise significance he places on this account. On occasions, he seems to be arguing in the following way: since the concept of a father is in part evaluative, since by a father we mean someone who is entitled to special consideration, then anyone who understands the concept of a father must also assent to the evaluations that go with it, must agree that those beings we call fathers are entitled to special consideration. If a man were to deny that fathers are entitled to special consideration then either he will have failed to understand what is meant by a father or he will have involved himself in a contradiction.

Now there have in fact been people who have wished to deny that fathers are entitled to special consideration. The Utilitarian Godwin argued that since the object of moral action is the benefit of mankind as a whole we should treat each individual as equal with every other and should avoid showing preference to particular classes of people, such as fathers. Preference, on Godwin's view, should be given only on the basis of principles which apply to all. 'I ought to prefer no human being to another, because that being is my father, my wife or my son, but because for reasons which equally appeal to all individuals that being is entitled to preference.'[1]

Melden sometimes seems to imply that Godwin's position might be dismissed as incoherent. Since what we mean by 'father' is someone to whom we owe special consideration, anyone who, like Godwin, denies that a father should be treated differently from anyone else is merely contradicting himself. The error in this line of argument may be indicated by referring, as Hare has done, to the concept of a nigger.[2] The concept of a nigger, like that of a father, is partly factual and partly evaluative. In calling someone a nigger one is not merely indicating the colour of his skin, one is also implying that he is the kind of person whom it is right to treat with contempt. Now if one wishes to hold that no category of persons should be singled out in this way as

[1] W. Godwin, *Political Justice*, Allen and Unwin 1890, II, 852.
[2] R. M. Hare, *Freedom and Reason*, p. 25.

specially deserving contempt, one is not deterred from doing so by being told that there exists a special category of persons who by definition deserve contempt, namely, niggers; one merely replies by saying that in this sense of nigger, no one deserves to be called a nigger. Someone might object by saying that the term nigger derives its sense from the complex institution of slavery, or from its use within a society such as that of the Southern States of America which has been affected by that institution, and that to understand the role of the nigger within the institution of slavery is to understand that he is a person who is to be treated with contempt. The answer to this objection is that it would have been better if that complex institution had never existed. Similarly, it would be no objection to Godwin's view to say that what we mean by a father is someone who is entitled to special consideration, for Godwin would have replied by saying that in this sense of father, no one should be treated as a father. Nor would it be an objection to say that the role of a father within the institution of the family is such that fathers are to be treated with special consideration, for Godwin, who thought badly of marriage and the institution of the family, would have replied by saying that it would have been better if that institution had never existed.

In fairness to Melden, it must be said that the above criticism of his view is based not so much on what he says as on what he seems to imply, and it is therefore possible that he would not wish to draw the consequences which we have attributed to him. Nevertheless, when in referring to the right of the father to special consideration he says that this right may be identified with the role of the father in the family, he makes it at least plausible to interpret him as saying that anyone who acknowledges the role must also acknowledge the right, that anyone who is familiar with the institution of the family is bound to admit that those beings whom we call fathers should be treated with special respect. There is, however, no doubt that this view is a mistaken one. Thus Godwin, who was born in England during the eighteenth century, was perfectly familiar with the institution of the family, yet he denied that fathers should be treated with special consideration. This reveals that a mere consideration of the institution of the family will not in itself entail that Godwin's opinion is incoherent.

Having recognised this, however, it is important not to fall into an opposing error. There is a temptation to suppose that if Godwin can reject certain values then those who do not reject these values must have decided at some time to accept them. But people who acknowledge the rights of parents do not have to decide in general to do so; they merely take part in the practices from which these rights follow naturally. They do not ask themselves whether the rights of parents ought to be considered.[1] To ask that question is already to place oneself outside the institution of the family and to have begun to question it. Now the point we should wish to make is that while it is possible to raise a question of this kind with regard to any particular institution or practice, it will always proceed from some further practice or practices to which the questioner is related in a manner comparable with that in which those who take part in family life, and recognise its values, are related to the institution of the family.

The alternative to recognising this point is to suppose, with Hare, that moral values are based ultimately on decision or choice. This view is not so very different from the view that moral values are based ultimately on personal intuitions. Common to both is the assumption that moral values come into our minds from nowhere and may be understood independently of the relations in which we stand to other people. But this is not the case. One can understand what Melden describes as the role of the father without acknowledging the father's rights, but one cannot genuinely acknowledge or *reject* his rights without understanding his role. This is because the rights of a father

---

[1] They might, of course, ask this question on a particular occasion; but we are thinking of the question raised in a general way, the way in which Godwin raised it in order to answer it in the negative.

depend on his position in the family not simply for their existence but also for their sense. Unless one were acquainted with family life, and with the father's position within that life, one would not know what one was doing in acknowledging or in rejecting the rights of a father. Furthermore any set of values which one can imagine will have a similar relation to some set of social conditions. This is why we have said that values are to be understood as they arise within ways of life, or, as we have described them, moral practices, which occur at definite times and at definite places. What makes moral choice possible is that any complex way of life will consist of a number of different practices and the values of one practice may be assessed in the light of another. Thus one is born into a family life, but the life of the family is not the whole of one's existence. One enters into wider activities having values which may not merely differ from but which may actually be opposed to those of the family. The reason why Hare's view is plausible is that, living in a complex society, one has the ability to look down on a particular practice and bring it beneath one's judgement and this makes it easy to suppose that one is oneself the source of one's moral values, that practices are to be judged by values which arise from one's own free choice or faculty of intuition.

The mistake in this view may be illustrated by considering why it is that Godwin's denial of a father's rights is intelligible.[1] The matter is complicated because Godwin is partly influenced by philosophical considerations of a utilitarian kind, but in the main his view would seem to rest on an appeal to justice or fairness. If one gives special consideration to one's parents one may well be ignoring the claims of people who are in greater need of one's help. One should therefore treat all people as equal, considering the needs of each as they arise, and not allow one's judgement to be moved by accidental factors. This is recognisably an

[1] It should be borne in mind that we are not committed to agreeing with Godwin's view, our aim being not to defend Godwin, but to show why his view is one with which it would be intelligible to disagree.

appeal to principles of justice which exert an influence in many areas of our lives. With regard to the law of the land, for example, we should say that it should apply equally to all people, that there should not be a special category of law which favours some classes of people, and a different, harsher, law for others. What Godwin is saying is that this principle should apply also in our dealings with our family; they, too, should be treated not with special favour, but exactly as we should treat everyone else. This view, whether or not one agrees with it, is certainly intelligible, but it is intelligible because it appeals to principles which people already apply and which are no more the product of decision than are the principles that are found in the life of the family. Godwin does not have to *decide* that justice is good but rather he makes his particular decision intelligible by appealing to justice, the goodness of which he takes for granted.[1] The ability to criticise values does not show that values are ultimately the product of our decisions alone, for criticism, no less than conformity, must derive its sense from the practices to which we belong.

[1] It is worth indicating that there is a further obvious connection between Godwin's principles and the social movement of his time. We are thinking of the social movement which led in the eighteenth century to the revolutions in France and America. The American Declaration of Independence reads, 'We hold these truths to be *self-evident*, that all men are created equal . . .'

Jefferson calls these 'truths' self-evident, because they are not the things he is seeking to justify, but are the principles by which the particular claim of independence is to be justified.

Moral Practices and Miss Anscombe's Grocer

Miss Anscombe's grocer[1] teaches moral philosophers a valuable lesson, namely, that there is no need to appeal to anything beyond the facts when considering what is morally important. No appeals to a mysterious realm of evaluative meaning are necessary. If a customer orders potatoes, and the grocer delivers them to him, the grocer is justified in saying that the customer owes him for the potatoes. There is little point in the philosophers' protest that we cannot derive an 'ought'—that he owes the grocer for the potatoes—from an 'is'—that he ordered the potatoes and that the grocer delivered them—since the example illustrates the artificiality of the thesis. It will not do either to say that the facts only hold within certain social institutions, since the facts have their *meaning* within the institution of buying and selling. The grocer can say that the man owes him money on the basis of the above facts, in the context of the above institution. Certain things have happened: a man has ordered potatoes and had them delivered; other things follow: he owes the grocer for the potatoes. This is not a new theory, but a familiar story. The umpire raises his finger and the batsman walks, the jury decides and a sentence is pronounced, the priest pronounces and the man and woman are married, etc. etc. All these facts have

[1] G. E. M. Anscombe, 'On Brute Facts', *Analysis* Vol. 18, 1957–58.

their meaning within certain institutions, but they do not describe these institutions; that is not what they tell us.

That the business transactions described have taken place is not absolute proof that a debt has been incurred, since the whole thing might be part of an amateur film production. What are we to say then? 'What is true is this: what ordinarily amounts to such-and-such a transaction *is* such-and-such a transaction, unless a special context gives it a different character'.[1] Normally, Miss Anscombe's grocer does not need to look for special circumstances. Most days it is business as usual. Those philosophers who insist on there being a gap between 'ought' and 'is' *in all circumstances*, fail to recognise the force of the normal implications of buying and selling, or the force of our normal ways of doing things.

But, having seen how much Miss Anscombe's grocer has to teach moral philosophers, we must also note the way in which he obscures important moral possibilities. This can be seen in at least two ways.

First, Miss Anscombe's grocer will not admit the possibility of serious moral or political rebellion against the institution of buying and selling. One day, an extraordinary day it is true, a man entered his shop, asked that potatoes be delivered to his house, but later denied that he owed the grocer anything. He claimed to have been protesting against the institution of buying and selling. The grocer pointed out, quite rightly, that a great deal is involved in the rebel's activity. The notion of contractual agreement runs deep in our society. We may share the grocer's doubts about how far such a rebel is going to get, but that is not the point at issue. There is something seriously wrong with a moral philosophy or a moral attitude which cannot, because of its presuppositions, recognise the seriousness of moral rebellion. Of course, not *any* rebellion will count as a moral rebellion. Lack of inclination will not count as a *moral* reason for rebellion against Miss Anscombe's grocer. The moral or political rebel will have a story to tell. He cannot

[1] ibid., p. 70.

be compared with the liar, who, far from wanting to destroy the practice of truth-telling, takes advantage of it and needs it in order to achieve his ends. The liar does not rebel, he manipulates. But the rebel will have a story to tell about moral and political ideals, and alternative policies. To deny the possibility of such a story is an indication of a lack of seriousness.

Second, and perhaps more important, Miss Anscombe's grocer's view of what people think ought to be done is a limited one. It is difficult to know to what extent he reflects Miss Anscombe's own view, so we had better talk about his views rather than hers. Miss Anscombe's grocer likes to know where he stands, and wants his customers to be aware of the same. One must be careful, however, in one's account of the grocer's limitations. If he were asked to justify his saying that the customer owed him money, his appeal would be to the rules of the game: 'You have ordered goods. I have delivered them. You owe me payment for them'. Normally, the grocer would go on to say, 'You must pay up'. In making this further move, the grocer does not appeal to anything beyond the facts. On the other hand, 'You must pay up" does not follow from the facts in the same way as the conclusion that the customer owes for the goods follows from the fact that the goods have been ordered and delivered. True, the fact that payment is made for goods delivered is not a merely contingent feature of the institution of buying and selling. Nevertheless, in certain situations, 'You must pay', viewed morally, may be regarded as a harsh demand rather than as a normal expectation. But would Miss Anscombe's grocer agree with this? It is tempting to think that he would not; that for him, once the goods have been ordered and delivered, the rest is obvious. But this would be a mistake.[1] The grocer's reac-

[1] This mistake appeared in my paper, 'Miss Anscombe's Grocer', *Analysis* July 1968 and was pointed out by Colwyn Williamson in 'Miss Anscombe's Grocer and Mr Phillips's Grocer' *Analysis* July 1968. For the reply to this latter paper see 'The Limitations of Miss Anscombe's Grocer', *Analysis* January 1969.

tion to all situations similar to the one described need not
be, 'You must pay up'. It is wrong to attribute to him the
view that moral truth consists in credit neither being asked
for nor given. This is not the source of the grocer's limitations. His views are limited, rather, because he thinks that
whatever his reaction is, it is the only moral possibility.

Things are different at the grocer's next door to Miss
Anscombe's flourishing businessman. He often says, 'Forget what you owe me' when his colleague says, 'You must
pay up'. He does not appeal to anything beyond the facts
either, but he gives them a different emphasis. It is these
different emphases that Miss Anscombe's grocer cannot
account for. He knows the rules of the game, and he wants
everyone to agree on what is fair or foul. He attracts all
those who like to know where they stand on moral matters,
and want everyone else to stand there too. Pharisees,
casuists, and those moral philosophers who deny that there
is a gap between 'ought' and 'is' *in all circumstances*, are
among his most frequent customers.

Things are more complex next door. All the facts known,
there is still room for a greater apprehension of them. There
is still a question of which facts are to be emphasised or
given priority. At this shop, there is always the possibility
of the poor, having ordered goods and had them delivered,
being told to forget their debts. Sometimes the shop is the
scene of heated moral disagreement, which often ends in
deadlock. Given that goods have been ordered and delivered and that the customer is temporarily unemployed,
people might well disagree about what ought to be done:
'Business is business'—'It's our duty to help'—'Charity
encourages laziness'—'Charity destroys self-respect'—'It
depends on how he spends his money'—'Did he become
unemployed through his own fault?'—'I don't know about
any of that, but forget what you owe me'—etc., etc.

Miss Anscombe's position seems to be this: if one wants
to understand a moral conclusion one can do so by seeing
how certain facts are brute relative to it. Thus, once we
understand that a man has ordered potatoes and had them

delivered, we can see that his owing for the potatoes consists in these facts. It might also be said that the grocer's saying, 'You ought to pay' consists in these facts, given that these are the only facts. Miss Anscombe recognises that a special context will put this business transaction in a new light, but she does not give examples. We have introduced a special consideration, namely, the fact that the debtor is unemployed. In the light of this fact there is nothing preventing Miss Anscombe's grocer from saying, 'Forget what you owe me'. But, now, applying her conception of 'brute facts' to the *new* situation and the *new* moral conclusion, Miss Anscombe would have to say that this moral conclusion consists in these facts which are brute relative to it. But this is precisely what the possibility of varied moral reactions shows to be mistaken. Given the new fact, the debtor's unemployment, some will conclude, 'You ought to pay up', and some will say, 'Forget what you owe me'. People may reach these conclusions for different reasons. But how can the variety of moral reactions to *the same* situation be analysed as Miss Anscombe suggests; how can the same facts be brute relative to *different* moral conclusions; how can the varied judgements simply consist in these facts? Miss Anscombe may say that she has no wish to apply her notion of 'brute facts' in these contexts. If so, the usefulness of the notion is extremely limited in moral philosophy, a fact which her original paper tends to obscure.

The possibility of varied moral reactions to the same facts is one of the most important features of the often confused philosophical insistence on the distinction between facts and values. The mere parading of facts will not always yield what we ought to do. Which facts do we consider important and how do we weigh them? These questions are an essential feature in the formation of moral attitudes. What cannot be denied is that facts which weigh a great deal for some people, do not weigh at all for others. It is important to recognise the diversity of moral possibilities. Otherwise, like Miss Anscombe's grocer, we shall tend to think that no moral seriousness exists in any place other than our own.

Of course, Miss Anscombe's grocer could change with changing situations. But Miss Anscombe's paper seems to suggest that whatever the situation, whatever changes it undergoes, there could only be one appropriate moral judgement—and that would be the judgement of her infallible grocer.

The Possibilities of Moral Advice

Professor Max Black tells us[1] that as a recognition of its remarkable philosophical influence, he proposes 'to assign to the principle that only factual statements can follow from exclusively factual statements the title "Hume's Guillotine" '.[2] He ends his paper by describing this principle as 'a dogma which ought by now to have been finally exploded'.[3] We assume that the 'by now' refers, not to the end of the article, but to the present state of contemporary moral philosophy, where the number of those prepared to assist in exploding the principle in question increases quarterly.

We want to consider the way in which Black thinks moral advice can be deduced from factual premisses. Certainly, in some contexts, it seems that one can argue from 'is' to 'should'. For example, as Black argues, if we know that *A* wants to checkmate his opponent *B* in a game of chess, and we see that he can only do so by moving the Queen, if *A* then asks us for advice, it follows that we *should* say 'Move the Queen'. But is there a transition from the chess example to an example of *moral* advice? Professor Black asks us to consider the following case:

[1] Max Black, 'The Gap Between "Is" and "Should" ', *Philosophical Review* LXXIII, 1964, pp. 165–81.
[2] ibid., p. 166.   [3] ibid., p. 181.

'*A*, playing chess with *B*, asks me for advice. I see that the one and only way to checkmate is to move the Queen and say "You should move the Queen". A bystander, *C*, however, who has overheard this, objects that *B* is in such precarious health that the shock of being suddenly mated by an inferior player might induce a stroke and kill him. *C*, therefore, says to *A*: "You should not move the Queen— perhaps you ought to break off the game". Is *C*'s advice or admonition in conflict with mine? If it is, I cannot properly argue that my advice follows from the two factual premises about *A*'s purpose and the necessary and sufficient condition for achieving it. For the addition of further premises—for example, about *B*'s state of health and the probable consequences to him of defeat—would produce a conclusion contrary to mine.'[1]

Black underestimates the significance of his own example. As a first reaction to it, he suggests that *C*'s comment involves a change of subject. The introduction of moral considerations takes one away from the question of what should be done *in this game*. We do not want to press the point here, but the distinction between games and morality is not as rigid as Black would make it. Consider, for example, the conflict between such attitudes as 'Win at all costs' and 'Observe the spirit of the game'. Black says that it is no doubt an important point that moral injunctions cannot be limited in the same way as advice on strategy during a game, but it is doubtful whether he has recognised the nature of the importance involved. Had he done so, he would not have tried to establish an analogy between advice in chess, granted the absence of so-called moral intrusions, and moral advice. In trying to do this he is guilty of serious confusions.

Black begins by stating that *within* a given context, such as a game, the way in which the question 'What should I do?' should be answered may be generally agreed upon. But given that you want to achieve *E* and that doing *M* is

[1] ibid., p. 175.

126

the one and only way of achieving E, does it follow as a logical necessity that you should do M? Black says that in the context of a game of chess, the facts already mentioned constitute a *conclusive* reason for doing M. We should not understand someone who, given the facts, advised 'You should not move the Queen'. The facts bind one to the *should*-conclusion as much as the facts bind one to a factual conclusion in an argument of the form 'P, if P then Q, therefore Q'. If someone said 'Therefore not-Q' in this context, we should be at a loss to know what he was up to.

Black is prepared to admit that there are differences between the two pieces of advice. For example, in the latter, to think P is also to think Q. Failure to think Q entails failure to understand P. Yet, it is not so in the case of a moral *should*-conclusion. Giving moral advice, unlike thinking Q given P, is a voluntary activity. A man may train himself to abstain from giving moral advice, or he may refrain from drawing a moral conclusion from the facts because of moral deficiency. For these reasons, Black is reluctant to say that the *should*-conclusion is entailed by the factual premisses. But once a man chooses to be involved in moral practices, the differences, for all practical purposes, are unimportant. Black says,

'If a moral conclusion is ever related to non-moral premisses in the fashion I have imagined, then, given that a moral conclusion is to be drawn, we have no choice as to what moral conclusion it shall be.'[1]

Clearly, the conclusion of this argument is false, and so is its initial hypothesis. To see this one need only elaborate a little on the situation in which advice is sought during a game of chess. As well as knowing of B's precarious health, and the probable effect of sudden defeat by an inferior player on him, let us suppose that various bystanders also know that B takes his chess very seriously indeed, and that he would be terribly upset if he thought that he had been 'given' a game; indeed, upset enough to induce a stroke.

[1] ibid., p. 178.

They also know, let us say, that *B* had been told by his doctor to give up playing chess because of the tension it caused in him, to which advice *B* had replied, 'In that case I'll die with my boots on'. *A* not only asks *C*, but all the bystanders, what he should do. They all know the facts we have mentioned, plus the fact that the only way to checkmate is to move the Queen. What advice should the bystanders give? Black tells us that 'The truth of the premisses restricts the performance, whether that of "advising" or something else, to a single possibility'.[1] Well, then, what is 'the single possibility' in the situation I have outlined?

If we ask, 'What advice *could* the bystanders give which would count as *moral* advice?' we can see that there are *many* possibilities. Here are some which come readily to mind.

Bystander *D* argues: 'What is more important than a man's life? After all, chess is only a game. I know that *B* has disregarded medical advice in order to play, but he is wrong in taking this attitude, and so I feel I am doing the right thing in overruling it. After all, he may never find out that he was given the game, whereas the consequences of his sudden defeat are very real. You should not move the Queen'.

Bystander *E* argues: 'How I admire *B*. He is one of the few who have seen through the shallowness of this life-at-all-costs attitude. What is life stripped of everything worthwhile? I do not share his passion for chess, but I understand it. I too should prefer to die with my boots on, rather than carry on in some kind of pretence. You should move the Queen'.

Bystander *F* argues: 'I agree with *B*. I understand him perfectly. We have played chess together for years. You should move the Queen'.

Bystander *G* argues: 'I disagree strongly with *B*'s attitude to his health, but I also think that every man has a right to his moral opinions. You should move the Queen'.

[1] ibid., p. 179.

Bystander *H* argues: 'I do not propose to give positive advice. A man's life may be at stake whatever you do. I am prepared to clarify the issues involved as I see them, but you must draw your own moral conclusion'.

All these are *moral* reactions. Whether one agrees with them or not is another matter. Of course, the situation can be far more complicated; by the introduction of the fact that *B* has a family, for instance. But given that the situation is as we have described it, what is 'the single possibility' to which the facts bind us? Black says,

'Given the truth of the factual premisses concerning a man's end and the necessary and sufficient condition for attaining that end, and given one is to make some second-person "should"-statement, one must say "You should do *M*"—and nothing else will do. What kind of a "must" is this? It seems to mean here precisely what "must" means when we say that anybody affirming the premisses of a valid deductive argument must also affirm that argument's conclusion. Choice of the given "should"-statement is enforced by the rules, understandings, or conventions governing the correct uses of "should" and other words occurring in the argument: nobody who understands the premisses of the practical argument and knows the rules for the proper use of "should" can honestly offer any other "should"-conclusion. In this respect, the parallel with "theoretical" arguments is strong. Accordingly, no special "practical" logic is needed in such cases: the relevant principles are the familiar ones employed throughout deductive reasoning.'[1]

The confusions in the above argument are due in part to a mistaken view of 'facts'. True, *within* a given moral viewpoint, the facts will bind those who share it to similar moral conclusions. But, for them, the facts already have moral import. It is not a case of moral conclusions being deduced from non-evaluative factual premisses. Black thinks that the facts bind one to moral advice which he regards as 'the single possibility' in the situation. But as

[1] ibid., p. 179.

we have tried to show in our five examples, the moral advice one thinks one ought to give will be determined by one's moral beliefs; it is such beliefs which give the facts their relevance and significance. There are no 'theoretical' rules for the 'proper' use of 'should' which make one piece of advice the only honest possibility. To talk of 'the proper use of "should" ' is simply to beg the question: to equate one's own moral views with 'the single possibility'. In case our five examples of possible moral advice in the above situation are interpreted as a sign of theoretical disinterestedness, we had better put our cards on the table and say that at the moment we do not know what advice ought to be given in the situation we have described, or whether positive advice should be given at all.

Another curious feature of Black's argument is his stress on a man's end and the necessary and sufficient condition for attaining that end. He thinks these facts bind one to a specific moral conclusion. Clearly, this is not the case. Morality does not wait on these facts. On the contrary, people's aims and their methods of attaining them wait on morality. A bystander would indicate his lack of moral concern if he advised *A* as follows: '*B*'s health is irrelevant. You want to win this game; that's all that matters. You can only checkmate by moving the Queen, so move it'. Again, it may be true that someone wants to extend his business, and that the one and only way of doing so is by ruining his friend's business. But morality says, 'Not that way'. On the other hand, where a person's aims and methods of attaining them are moral, it is always possible, as we have seen, for someone else to disagree and put forward other moral proposals. There are no 'single possibilities'.

Finally, a word about the challenge Professor Black puts to his readers at the end of his paper. He says,

'Once Hume's Guillotine has been discredited, we may hope to find more important arguments containing valid transitions from "is" to "should" or from "is" to "ought". If I am not mistaken, the following argument from factual premisses to a moral conclusion is valid:

'Doing A will produce pain.

'Apart from producing the pain resulting from A, doing A will have the same consequences that not doing A would have had.

'Therefore, A ought not to be done'.[1]

On one interpretation, the conclusion of this argument can be shown to be false. If by 'consequences' Professor Black means the kind of thing Mill had in mind, it is clear that many people have thought that they ought to do A on moral grounds despite the absence of such consequences. For example, a man may feel that he ought to die for a cause although the cause is lost. Again, a soldier may refuse to give details of plans to the enemy under torture, although he may know that they have already discovered them. Such actions can certainly be given a *moral* point, though in Mill's sense they would be pointless.

But Black may want to include in his 'consequences' the agent's regard for his moral convictions (as opposed to the success or failure which may attend standing by them), and his remorse at failing in the time of trial. The second premiss of Black's argument could then be reworded as follows: 'Apart from producing the pain resulting from A, doing A will have the same point that not doing A would have had'. The challenge is then to show that pointless pain has a point. No wonder Professor Black feels confident about the argument! But confidence is bought at the price of triviality. Certainly, Hume's point is unaffected by the argument. Black tells us that pointless pain is bad, but this is to say nothing at all, since the whole moral issue concerns *what is to count* as pointless pain, and this is not something that the facts will tell us. There will be moral disagreement over what is and what is not to count as pointless. Is dying for a lost cause pointless? Black's second premiss, once it is given a *positive* content, will be a premiss which already has moral import; that is, it will say that such-and-such is pointless. Those who disagree about this pointlessness will

[1] ibid., p. 180.

131

not feel bound to the moral conclusion. There are no deductive moves to 'single possibilities' which will change this situation.

Morality is not a game, and philosophers are not people who have special insight into its 'rules'. We think Professor Black ought to take another look at Hume's Guillotine, for, unless we are mistaken, his arguments are on the block.

Index

Index